Acing Interviews

FOR

DUMMIES®

PORTABLE EDITION

D1167592

Acing Interviews

FOR

DUMMIES®

PORTABLE EDITION

by **Joyce Lain Kennedy**

WILEY

John Wiley & Sons, Inc.

Acing Interviews For Dummies®, Portable Edition

Published by
John Wiley & Sons, Inc.
111 River St.
Hoboken, NJ 07030-5774
www.wiley.com

For general information on our other products and services, please contact our Customer Care Department within the U.S. at 877-762-2974, outside the U.S. at 317-572-3993, or fax 317-572-4002.

For technical support, please visit www.wiley.com/techsupport.

Wiley publishes in a variety of print and electronic formats and by print-on-demand. Some material included with standard print versions of this book may not be included in e-books or in print-on-demand. If this book refers to media such as a CD or DVD that is not included in the version you purchased, you may download this material at http://booksupport.wiley.com. For more information about Wiley products, visit www.wiley.com.

ISBN 978-1-118-30704-5 (pbk); ISBN 978-1-118-30705-2 (ebk); ISBN 978-1-118-30706-9 (ebk); ISBN 978-1-118-30707-6 (ebk)

Manufactured in the United States of America

10 9 8 7 6 5 4 3 2

Publisher's Acknowledgments

Technical Adviser: James M. Lemke

Project Editor: Jennifer Tebbe

Composition Services: Indianapolis Composition Services Department

Cover Photo: © iStockphoto.com/porcorex

WILEY

Table of Contents

Introduction... *1*

About This Book 1
Conventions Used in This Book 1
Foolish Assumptions 3
Icons Used in This Book.. 3
Where to Go from Here 4

Chapter 1: An At-a-Glance Guide to the Modern Job Interview 5

Putting Your Best Self Forward 6
Surveying the Contemporary Interviewing Scene 7
Technology changes the game...................................... 7
New kinds of interviewers are in the mix 8
The "job-hopper objection" poses a hurdle................ 8
The loyalty oath doesn't mean what it used to 9
Small-business jobs call for a different approach 10
Storytelling skills are valuable 10
Fitting in can mean all the difference......................... 11
Seven Concepts to Get You Hired.. 12
Go all out in planning ahead... 12
Distinguish screening from selection interviews 12
Verify early what they want and
show how you can deliver 13
Connect all your qualifications
with a job's requirements...................................... 14
Memorize short-form sales statements
about yourself 14
Win two thumbs up from the hiring
manager, and you're in!.. 15
Try not to talk money until you know they want you 16
Tactics for Winning Over Any Interviewer 17
Play the likeability card 17
Style your body language 17
Be a treat: Act upbeat.. 18
Start your interview on the right foot 18
Remember that you have a speaking part.................. 18
Revisit the dramatic pause.. 19
Agree to take pre-employment tests 19

Flesh out your story beyond a college degree........... 19
Bring a pen and notebook with you 20
Keep your ears up and your eyes open 20

Chapter 2: Getting Past Screening Interviews 23

The Scoop on Screening Interviews 23
Surveying Some Common Screening Questions 24
Presenting the Three Types of Screening Styles 25
Being Prepared for Live Phone Screens............................... 26
Stock your back-stage office with essentials............. 26
Make phone appointments... 26
Project your winning image... 27
Acing Automated Phone Screens... 29
Pushing the Right Buttons: Computer Screens.................... 31

Chapter 3: Surveying the Many Styles of Interviews.... 33

Mastering Interviews by Interviewer...................................... 33
One-to-one interview 34
Group interview 34
Serial interview 35
Mastering Interviews by Technique 35
Behavior-based interview.. 36
Directive interview 39
Nondirective interview 40
Stress interview 40
Mastering Interviews at Remote Locations 43
Mealtime interview 43
Job fair interview 46

Chapter 4: Answering Questions with Ease..........47

Telling Someone about Yourself 48
Answering Questions Related to the
Job, Company, and Industry... 55
Answering Questions about Your Skills............................... 58
Making Your Experience Relevant... 63
Dealing with the Premature Salary Question 70
Stalling money talk the smart way.............................. 71
Knowing market pay rates just in case...................... 74
Handling Questions about a Special Situation 75
When you've long been in the same job..................... 75
When you're shoved out the door................................ 77
When sexual orientation is up for discussion........... 78
When you've worked everywhere 80

When gaps drill holes in your history......................... 82
When you're demoted a notch.................................... 83
Answering a Questionable Question 84
Defining illegal questions.. 85
Defining inappropriate questions............................... 86
Rehearsing dicey questions 86

Chapter 5: Asking the Right Questions at the Right Times..............................89

Asking Selling Questions before the Offer 90
Drawing Out Hidden Objections 91
Treading Lightly around Employer-
Performance Questions.. 92

Chapter 6: Closing on a High Note 93

Making a Strategic Exit... 93
Your parting sales pitch 94
Leaving the door open 96
Follow Up or Fall Behind.. 97
Letters 97
E-mail.. 98
Telephone calls... 99
Your After-Interview Checklist....................................... 101

Chapter 7: Be in the Know before You Go..........103

What Online Searches Reveal.. 104
Using Specific Questions to Focus Your Research............. 105
Size and growth patterns.. 105
Direction and planning... 105
Products or services 106
Competitive profile... 106
Culture and reputation... 106
Company financials 107
Ready, Aim, Fact-Find.. 107

Chapter 8: Practicing for the Big Day 113

Taking Steps to Calm Your Nerves 113
Practicing with a Video Recorder.. 116
Unlocking the Power of Body Language 117
Make Like an A-List Candidate 121
Anticipating Interview Trapdoors 121
Disruptions 121
Silent treatment 122

Chapter 9: Dressing the Part 123

You Are What You Wear 123
Dressing to Fit the Job and the Job's Culture 124
Selecting from the Basic Types of Interview Wardrobes.....126
Remaining conservative... 127
Cruising business casual 128
Working in casual wear.. 131
Selecting creative fashion... 132

Chapter 10: Welcome to the 21st Century Video Interview 135

Getting Familiar with the Three Basic Models 136
Working with third-party vendors............................. 136
Chatting through Skype 137
Videoconferencing services 138
Rocking the Video Job Interview 138
Getting ready to video interview 139
During the interview... 140

Chapter 11: Ten Tips for Interviewing Success 143

Make Conversation 143
Remember Your True Goal..................................... 143
Leave the Begging to Others 144
Be a Respectful Equal in the Discussion 144
Show Confidence from the Get-Go......................... 144
Avoid Ad Libbing Ad Infinitum 145
Realize the Interviewer Isn't Your New Best Friend.......... 145
Know That Faulty Assumptions
Equal Faulty Interviewing...................................... 145
Keep Emotions out of the Interview 146
Ask Questions That Show You Care Where You Go.......... 146

Index *147*

Introduction

● ●

*A*lthough much has changed in the world of job inter-views, such as the rise of social media that changes what privacy means and the increasingly popular video interview, what hasn't changed is the fundamental role job interviews play in the employment process. Job interviews continue to be those crucial meetings that seal the deal on who gets hired and who gets left on the outside looking in.

If you'd rather fight off an alien invasion than be grilled in an interview, take heart — you've come to the right guidebook. With the help of dozens of interviewing authorities, I make your interviewing challenge easy and successful.

About This Book

A guidebook of contemporary interview arts, *Acing Interviews For Dummies,* Portable Edition, contains the distilled wisdom of hundreds of leading interview experts whose brains I've been privileged to pick for many years. By absorbing the guid-ance and tips I pass on in this guide, you can interview your way into a job by outpreparing and outperforming the other candidates.

Conventions Used in This Book

To assist your navigation of this guidebook, I employ the fol-lowing conventions:

- ✔ **Bold** text denotes keywords and action steps to take.

- ✔ *Italics* highlight either new words or terms I define (although I also occasionally use them for emphasis).

- ✔ Web addresses appear in `monofont` to distinguish them from the regular type in the paragraph.

I also use the following terminology to label specific roles and organizations:

- ✔ A *candidate* or *job seeker* is a person applying for a job. (Another once-common label, *applicant*, is used less today because of a federal regulation that defines an applicant as one to be counted in discrimination monitoring. But *applicant* means the same thing.)

- ✔ An *interviewer* is someone interviewing a candidate for a job. An *interviewee* is a candidate being interviewed for a job.

- ✔ A *human resources* (or *HR*) *specialist, HR manager,* or *screener* is an employer sentry who is conducting a screening (preliminary) interview.

  A *hiring manager, hiring authority, decision maker, decision-making manager,* or *department manager* is a management representative who is conducting a selection interview and who has the authority to actually hire a person for a specific position.

- ✔ A *company, employer,* or *organization* is the entity you hope to work for, whether private and profit-making, or private and nonprofit. *Agency* implies employment in the government (public) sector.

- ✔ A *recruiter* (also called a *headhunter*) is an intermediary between the employer and you. *Internal recruiters* work inside the company, either as regular employees of the human resources department or as contract employees. *Third-party recruiters* or *independent recruiters* are external recruiters, some of whom are employed as retained recruiters on an ongoing basis, while most are employed on a transaction basis as contingency recruiters and are paid only when a candidate they submit is hired.

- ✔ A *career coach* (also called a *career consultant)* helps job seekers gain workplace opportunities. (A *career counselor* and a career coach represent two different professions, although their work sometimes overlaps.)

- ✔ A *hiring professional* is any of the aforementioned professionals who's engaged internally or externally in the employment process.

Foolish Assumptions

In addition to being someone who needs reliable interviewing information that you can consume while on the go, I assume you picked up this book for one of the following reasons:

- ✔ You've never been through a competitive interview and you're freaking out. You need a couple thousand friendly pointers from someone who's interviewed many of the marquee minds in the job interview business and lived to write about it.

- ✔ You've been through a competitive interview and assume the company sank like Atlantis because you never heard a peep from those folks again. Or maybe you could have done better and actually heard back if you'd known more about what you were doing in this interview thing.

- ✔ The most important interview of your career is coming up. You realize that now is the hour to dramatically improve your interviewing skills. You need help, and you're willing to learn and work for success.

- ✔ You've been through a slew of job interviews over the course of your career and have a hunch that some important things have changed (you just don't know what exactly). You want to catch up with the help of a trusted resource.

Icons Used in This Book

For Dummies signature icons are the little round pictures you see in the margins of the book. I use them to focus your attention on key bits of information. Here's a list of the icons you can expect to find:

This icon signals situations in which you can find trouble if you don't make a good decision.

This icon flags news you can use that you won't want to forget.

This icon lets you in on interviewing best practices.

Where to Go from Here

On the stress scale of life, job interviewing ranks with making a speech before 500 people when you can't remember your name or why you're standing in a spotlight at a podium. The spot where you start in this guidebook depends on your present needs:

- ✔ When you have a job interview tomorrow, quickly read Chapter 1 for an overview, followed by Chapter 11 for an instant infusion of key know-how. Additionally, go to the company's website to glean as much basic information as you can and don't forget to read the company's press releases.

- ✔ When you have a few days before you're scheduled for an interview, read Chapter 1 and then flip through the Table of Contents to find the chapters that deal with your most pressing concerns. Pay attention to Chapter 6, which reveals how to stack the deck in your favor during the closing minutes of your interview.

- ✔ When you have plenty of time, read the book from cover to cover. Practice recommended strategies and techniques. After you master the information in these pages, you'll have a special kind of insurance policy that pays big dividends for as long as you want to work.

For even more information about job interviews, pick up a copy of *Job Interviews For Dummies,* 4th Edition, from www. dummies.com or your local bookseller.

Chapter 1

An At-a-Glance Guide to the Modern Job Interview

In This Chapter

▶ Focusing on making a good impression rather than "being natural"

▶ Discovering what's new in interviewing

▶ Zeroing in on seven secrets to interview success

▶ Charming interviewers, each and every time

A resume or profile functions as bait to snag a job inter-view. The interview is the decisive event when a hiring authority decides whether you'll be offered the job.

Because the job interview is the single most important part of getting a job — and because you may not have interviewed in awhile — any number of unfortunate scenarios may be sneaking into your subconscious, including fears of these confidence-disturbers:

✔ Stumbling and mumbling your way through the ordeal

✔ Being glued to a hot seat as they sweat the answers out of you

✔ Forgetting your interviewer's name (or the last place you worked)

Exhale. You've come to the right book. Take the suggestions within these pages to heart, and you'll head into every inter-view feeling confident, calm, and well prepared. What more can you ask?

Putting Your Best Self Forward

Like reality shows on TV, interviews are based on reality but, in fact, are staged. Consequently, the age-old advice to "be yourself" and "be natural" doesn't always lead to employment.

When it comes to being yourself, you may wear many hats in your day-to-day life — father, daughter, public speaker, long-time volunteer, top salesperson, marathon runner, short-order cook, coin collector. But if you're reading this, you're either about to put on the hat of job seeker or you're already wearing it. Consequently, you want to focus your attention on that hat so that you appear to be a hard-charging job seeker. To do less than that is to court unemployment — or underemployment.

As for being natural, that's fine so long as you don't use your desire to be natural and authentic as an excuse to display your warts or blurt out negative characteristics.

 Never treat a job interview as a confessional in which you're obligated to disclose imperfections, indiscretions, or personal beliefs that don't relate to your future job performance.

Job interviews are time-centric. Every minute counts in the getting-to-know-you game. And to really know someone in a brief encounter of 15, 30, or 60 minutes is simply impossible. Instead of real life, each participant in an interview sees what the other participant(s) wants seen. If you doubt that, think back: How long did you need to really get to know your roommate, spouse, or significant other?

If you insist on being natural, an employer may pass you over because of your unkempt beard or unshined shoes, or because you don't feel like smiling that day.

The things you've done to date — your identification of your skills, your resume and profile, your cover letter, your networking, your social media efforts — all are wasted if you fail to deliver a job interview that produces a job offer.

Because you have so little time to make the right impression, maximize your critical brief encounters by mastering the skills of storytelling, using body language, and establishing rapport. Not sure where to start? Relax. I provide the essential pointers in this modern interview guide.

Surveying the Contemporary Interviewing Scene

Are you having trouble staking out your future because you can't close the sale during job interviews? This mangled proverb states the right idea:

If at first you don't succeed . . . get new batteries.

Recharge yourself with knowledge of the new technology and trends that are affecting job interviews. Here are highlights of the contemporary job interview space.

Technology changes the game

Classic interviewing skills continue to be essential to job search success, but more technology firepower is needed in a world that's growing increasingly complex, interconnected, and competitive.

The new tech trends revolutionize all components of the job search, including the all-important job interview. Following is a rundown of two key technological newcomers and how they change interviewing practices:

- **Video job interviews:** Both live and recorded video job interviews are coming of age, requiring that you acquire additional skills and techniques to make the cut. Chapter 10 is a primer on how you can outflank your competition by presenting like a pro in video interviews.

- **Automated screening interviews:** Automated and recorded phone screening services permit employers to ask up to a dozen canned screening questions and allow candidates up to two minutes to answer each question. Informed interviewees anticipate the questions and must hit their marks the first time because there are no do-overs on recorded answers. Read about this technology in Chapter 2.

New kinds of interviewers are in the mix

If the last time you trod the boards of job interviewing you went one to one with a single interviewer, usually a white man or woman, get ready for a different set of questioners, like these possibilities:

- A veteran team of six managers — individually or collectively
- A hiring manager (especially in technical and retail fields) who is two decades younger than you
- Someone of another color or heritage

The "job-hopper objection" poses a hurdle

The current employer-driven job market makes it easy for companies to buy into the "job-hopper objection" and, as a matter of policy, turn away unemployed candidates and people who've held three jobs in five years. Unfortunately, many of these automatic rejects have been trapped in a cycle of frequent layoffs, part-time work, temp assignments, seasonal employment, contract jobs, freelance gigs, and company shutdowns.

Some companies refuse to hire so-called job hoppers, claiming they'll quit before employers can get a return on their training investment — or that, if the unemployed candidates were any good, they'd be on someone's payroll.

What's a sincere, hard-working person to do? Try this quartette of basic rebuttals:

- **Say varied experience beats repeated experience.** Explain how your dynamic work history makes you a far more vibrant and resourceful contributor than if you'd been stationary for four years.

- ✔ **Briefly explain departures.** Give a reasonable, short, even-toned account of why you left each job. (It wasn't your fault.)

- ✔ **Review your accomplishments.** You can't change the amount of time you were on certain jobs, but you can divert the focus to your accomplishments and contributions. Employers are impressed by candidates who are good at what they do, even if they had only a short period of time in the role.

- ✔ **Confirm interest in stable employment.** Forget the "loyalty" chatter. Make a point of your intense interest in a stable opportunity where you can apply all your considerable know-how for the employer's benefit.

Chapter 4 offers more suggestions on how to maximize the value of your experience.

The loyalty oath doesn't mean what it used to

Answers to certain questions are pretty much the same year after year, but watch out for one humdinger requiring a new response: Why do you want to work here? The old "I'm looking for a home and I'll be loyal to you forever" statements don't play as well as they once did.

Many employers now solicit contract employees — no muss, no fuss in getting them out the door when a project's finished or when a decision is made to outsource the work.

Rather than pledge eternal fidelity, talk about your desire to do the work. Talk about how you're driven to funnel substantial amounts of productivity into the job quickly. Talk about wanting to use your superior technology skills. Talk about your interest in work that excites you, work that matters.

But fidelity? Pass on that as a theme song; it won't make the charts today.

Stock up on what you *should* say instead of talking about loyalty in Chapter 4.

Small-business jobs call for a different approach

Have you grown up professionally in a large-company environment? If so, carefully consider the answers you give when applying to small companies. Such a move can happen sooner than you think if you're forced into an involuntary change of employment. Prime-timers in countless droves are discovering that the small company sector is where the action is for them.

Emphasize different aspects of your work personality than the ones you emphasize when interviewing for a big company. Interviewers at big companies and small companies have different agendas.

Owners of small business ventures may reject former big-company people because they think of people who come out of Big Corporate America as being

- ✔ Unaware of the needs of small business
- ✔ Too extravagant in their expectations of resources and compensation
- ✔ Too spoiled to produce double the work product their former jobs required
- ✔ Unwilling to wear more than one job hat at a time
- ✔ Deadwood, or they wouldn't have been cut loose from the big company

Storytelling skills are valuable

Behavior-based interviewing is said to predict future performance based on past performance in similar situations. The behavioral interviewing style isn't new, but it seems to be more popular than ever.

Advocates of the behavioral style claim that it's 55 percent predictive of future on-the-job behavior, compared to traditional interviewing, at only 10 percent predictive. The reasoning is, "If you acted a certain way once, you'll act that way again." Solid proof of this claim is hard to come by. But for you as a job seeker, it doesn't matter the least bit whether the claim is true or false. The behavioral style is such a big deal with employers today that you need to know how to use the style to your advantage.

It works like this: Interviewers ask candidates to tell them a story of a time when they reacted to a certain situation. *How did you handle an angry customer? Describe an example of a significant achievement in your last job.* The more success stories you can drag in from your past, the more likely the interviewers using this approach will highly rate your chances of achieving equivalent success in the future.

Fitting in can mean all the difference

"We chose another candidate who is a better job fit" is a familiar reason that seems to be heard today more often than before when explaining to a disappointed job seeker why someone else got the job.

In the workplace, "fit" essentially refers to how an individual fits into a company's culture. Company culture is expressed in the values and behaviors of the group, which forms a kind of "tribe" or, to use an analogy from high school, an "in crowd."

The culture typically flows from company or department chieftains: If the boss wears long sleeves, you wear long sleeves; if the boss shows a sense of humor, you show a sense of humor; if the boss works until 6 o'clock, you work until 6 o'clock.

When you're given the not-the-best-fit-for-the-job rejection, the reason is a

✔ Convenient, short, and legally safe answer

✔ Cover story

✔ Belief that the hiring decision makers perceive you won't fit in well with the "tribe"

When the reason really is the fit issue, decision makers may think that you can do the job but that you won't do it the way they want — and, furthermore, they just don't feel at ease with you.

Instead of losing sleep over a fit-based turn-down, move on. Do better pre-interview research (see Chapter 7). At least you won't waste time on companies well known for being a fortress of round holes when you're a square peg.

Seven Concepts to Get You Hired

You've heard it said over and over that you have only one chance to make a first impression. It's especially true for job interviewing, so make that first impression pay off. Read these seven super tips to make the hiring gods choose you at job interviews.

Go all out in planning ahead

Preparation makes all the difference in whether you get the best offers as you face intense scrutiny, field probing questions, and reassure employers who are afraid of making hiring mistakes. You must show that you're tuned in to the company's needs, that you have the skills to get up to speed quickly, and that you're a hand-in-glove fit with the company.

Fortunately, never in history has so much information about companies and industries been so easily accessible, both in print and online. Chapter 7 gives tons of tips on conducting pre-interview research.

Distinguish screening from selection interviews

As hiring action is increasingly concentrated in smaller companies, the separation between screening and selection interviews fades: The same person may do both types. But traditionally, here's how the types differ:

- ✔ **Screening interviews:** In large organizations, interviewing is usually a two-stage process. A screening specialist eliminates all candidates except the best qualified. The screening interview is usually conducted by telephone or video interviews instead of face-to-face in the same room. Survivors are passed to a manager (or panel of managers) who selects the winning candidate.

Screeners are experienced interviewers who look for reasons to screen you out based on your qualifications. Screeners can reject, but they cannot hire. They won't pass you on to hiring managers if your experience and education don't meet the specifications of the job.

When you're being interviewed by a screener, be pleasant and neutral. Volunteer no strong opinions. Raise no topics, except to reinforce your qualifications. Answer no questions that aren't asked — don't look for trouble. But do remember to smile a lot.

✔ **Selection interviews:** By the time you're passed on to a hiring authority who makes the selection, you're assumed to be qualified or you wouldn't have made it that far along the channels of employment. You're in a pool of "approved" candidates chosen for the selection interview.

At a selection interview, move from neutral into high gear if the person doing the interview will be your boss or colleague. No more bland behavior — turn up the wattage on your personality power. This is the best time to find out whether you'll hit it off with the boss or colleagues, or fit into the company culture.

Verify early what they want and show how you can deliver

Almost as soon as you're seated in a selection interview, ask the interviewer to describe the scope of the position and the qualifications of the ideal person for it. Then use this information to confirm what you discovered in your research (see Chapter 7). If you're wrong, you want to know immediately that you need to shift direction.

Confirming your research (or gaining this information on the spot) is the key to the entire interview. You now know for sure the factors upon which the hiring decision is made and how to target your answers.

How can you adapt the tell-me-what-you-want tip when you're dealing with multiple interviewers? That's easy: Direct your question to the senior panel member and wait for an answer. Then gaze around the group and ask, "Does anyone have something to add to the ideal person description?"

Connect all your qualifications with a job's requirements

If a quick glance at your notes reminds you that the interviewer missed a requirement or two listed in the job posting when describing the position's scope and the ideal person for it, help the interviewer by tactfully bringing up the missing criteria yourself. Keep it simple:

> *I see from my notes that your posting asked for three years of experience. I have that and two years more, each with a record of solid performance in. . . .*

You want to demonstrate that you take this job possibility seriously, an attitude that the employer will applaud. Winning job offers by targeting your interview performance to a company's requirements is a logical follow-up to the resume targeting strategy that I explain in my book *Resumes For Dummies,* 6th Edition (Wiley).

Memorize short-form sales statements about yourself

Almost certainly, you will be asked to respond to some version of the "tell me about yourself" question (see Chapter 4). You're not helping your hiring chances if you respond with a question that a 13-year-old might ask: "What do you want to know?" That naive approach makes you sound unprepared.

Instead, commit to memory a short-form sales statement (two minutes max, and preferably less than one minute) that describes your education, experience, and skills, and matches your strengths to the jobs you seek.

Some people call such a statement a "commercial;" others prefer the terms "elevator speech" or "profile summary." Whatever you call it, after briefly reciting the facts of your background, make your statement sizzle by adding a couple personality sentences about such traits as your curiosity, commitment, and drive to succeed.

The "personal branding brief" is another version of the short-form sales statement. Used chiefly by professionals, managers, and executives, it's incorporated into all self-marketing opportunities, including job interviewing.

In personal branding, you become known for something — Jon Stewart for political satire and Serena Williams for tennis, for example. You don't have to be famous to pursue personal branding, but you do have to be consistent in your efforts to develop your brand.

Your goal is to perfect a *branding brief* that tells your "story" — one that rolls off your tongue — in about 20 to 30 seconds, or in 100 words or less:

> *After I graduated from San Diego State University, I worked in the insurance industry until I took a break to start a family. That accomplished, I went back for refresher education. Now, thoroughly updated, I'm looking for a new connection in either the insurance or financial fields.*

 The difference between a commercial and a branding brief is length and content. A commercial is longer and includes more details than a cut-to-the-chase branding brief.

Win two thumbs up from the hiring manager, and you're in!

Likeability is a huge factor in choosing and keeping employees, as I note later in this chapter. Given a choice of technically qualified applicants, employers almost always choose the one they like best. For your purposes, remember this:

> *We like people who are like us.*

How do you encourage the interviewer to think, "You and me against the problem" rather than "You against me"? Beyond exchanging pleasantries, establishing mutual interests, connecting with eye contact, and other well-known bonding techniques, watch for special opportunities.

 ✔ Suppose your interviewer looks harried, with ringing telephones and people rushing about interrupting your talk. Flash a sympathetic smile and commiserate: *It looks like you're having one of those days.* The subtext of your comment is, *I understand your frustrations. I've been in a similar place. You and I are alike.*

✔ Or suppose you're showing a work sample. Ask if you can come around to the interviewer's side of the desk to discuss your sample. You are looking at it "together."

Forget about age, color, gender, or ethnic background. Do whatever you reasonably can to make the hiring manager believe the two of you are cut from similar cloth.

Try not to talk money until you know they want you

When the salary question comes up at the beginning of an interview, say that money isn't your most important consideration — nor should it be at this point.

Admittedly, stalling salary talk until a better time is much more difficult today than it was a decade ago. But you should be holding out for the market value of the new job, not settling for an inadequate figure of your present or previous employment.

Only when you know the scope of the position and its market value — and that the company wants to hire you — are the stars in alignment to bargain in your best interest.

Winning candidates are memorable

Comparing TV reality talent show winners to job interview candidates, Phoenix career coach Joe Turner (www.jobchangesecrets.com) says it's the total package that counts. "You don't have to be the best singer or dancer — just the *most remembered* decent performer. Same for the job interview. You don't always have to be the best candidate with the top skills. You do have to find a way to be the *most remembered* hirable candidate."

Tactics for Winning Over Any Interviewer

Rookie? Prime-timer? Clerk? Chief executive officer? No matter. You can do exceptionally well by applying certain tactics that succeed in any interview scene. Some of these suggestions are basic and familiar, but most people who haven't been on the interview tour for awhile can use the reminders.

Play the likeability card

When you're up against a rigid requirement that you absolutely can't meet and that you're pretty sure is going to mean curtains for you in the interview, try this last-ditch compensatory response:

> *Let's say that you were to make me an offer and I accept. What can I do when I start to further compensate for my lack of [requirement] as I work hard to relieve your immediate workload?*

Essentially, you're counting on your likeability. You're asking the employer to revert to the philosophy of hiring for attitude and training for skill. You're using the likeability qualification to plug your requirement gap.

Style your body language

Interviewers observe not only your dress and interview answers but also your body language, facial expressions, posture, carriage, and gestures. If you're a rookie, think dignity. If you're a prime-timer, think energy. In between? Watch political candidates on TV for hints of what looks good and what doesn't.

Confirm that your body language is sending the "Hire me!" message with the tips in Chapter 8. Chapter 9's up-to-date data on dress and appearance add even more nonverbal firepower to your candidacy.

Be a treat: Act upbeat

Steer clear of negative words (such as *hate, absolutely not,* and *refuse*). And avoid such risky topics as the knock-down, drag-out fights you had with that bonehead you used to work for — never knock the old boss. Your prospective new boss may empathize with your old boss and decide to never be your boss at all.

Start your interview on the right foot

Here are four tips to help you make a good impression right off the bat:

✔ Find out in advance what to wear (see Chapter 9) and where the interview site is located. Make a trial run, if necessary.

✔ Be on time, be nice to the receptionist, read a business magazine while you're waiting, and — surprise, surprise — don't smoke, chew gum, or otherwise look as though you lack couth.

✔ Develop a couple icebreaker sound bites, such as comments about a nice office, attractive color scheme, or interesting pictures.

✔ Don't sit until you're asked or until the interviewer sits. Don't offer to shake hands until the interviewer does.

During the interview, frequently use the interviewer's name (but never use a first name unless you're old friends). And remember to make a lot of eye contact by looking at the bridge of an interviewer's nose. (Divert your gaze occasionally, unless you want to be perceived as more creepy than honest.)

Remember that you have a speaking part

Communication skills are among the most desired qualities employers say they want. Answer questions clearly and completely. Be sure to observe all social skills of conversation — no interrupting, no profanity. Just as you shouldn't limit yourself to one- or two-word answers, neither should you try to cover your nervousness with surround-sound endless talking. Aim for a happy medium.

Revisit the dramatic pause

In face-to-face live interviews, allowing a few moments of silence to pass, perhaps pausing to look at the ceiling or glance out an open window — taking time to think — can make you look wise and measured in your response. Pauses can raise the ante by reflecting disappointment in a salary offer. Pauses can suggest that you're reluctant to travel 50 percent of the time but that you're a team player and will consider the requirement.

A pause is effective body language and works great in live, face-to-face interviews. But today's interviewer may call on a telephone or use online video interviewing, and dead air time can make you appear dull-witted rather than contemplative. Here's the moral of the story: Exercise judgment in using the reflective pause as a communications tool. (When you just don't know the answer immediately, that's another story; stall by asking for clarification.)

Agree to take pre-employment tests

No one likes those annoying pre-employment tests. Job seekers keep hoping they'll drop off the face of the earth, but they're with us still. When you want the job, you're going to have to suck it up and test when asked. No test, no job.

Flesh out your story beyond a college degree

Education is a fulcrum for movement throughout your career, but relying on it alone to pull you through a competitive job search is a mistake. The mistake grows larger with too many mentions of an illustrious alma mater, assuming that the school's marquee power is a hall pass to move forward. For example, a couple mentions of Harvard in an interview are plenty; interviewers get it the first time. They wonder whether the Harvard background is the singular "accomplishment" a candidate offers.

Spell out your accomplishments with true examples — what you learned and what you can do with your degree that benefit the employer.

In marketing a three-dimensional you, think of your education as one dimension, your experience as a second dimension, and your accomplishment record as a third dimension. All are important.

Bring a pen and notebook with you

Making a note here and there is advisable, as long as you don't attempt to record a transcript. To illustrate, you want to jot down reminders to get back to the interviewer when you can't answer a question from memory.

Writing down what someone says is flattering to the speaker.

Keep your ears up and your eyes open

Don't just sell, sell, sell. Take time to listen. When you're constantly busy thinking of what you're going to say next, you miss vital points and openings. So work on your listening skills. When you don't understand an interviewer's question, ask for clarification.

Observe the interviewer's moves. Watch for three key signs: high interest (leaning forward), boredom (yawning or displaying a glazed look), or a devout wish to end the interview (stacking papers or standing up). After assessing where you stand with the interviewer, take the appropriate action:

✔ High interest suggests you're on the right track and should continue.

✔ The remedy for boredom is to stop and ask, *Would you rather hear more about (whatever you've been talking about) or my skills in the ABC area?*

✔ When the interviewer is ready to end the meeting, first ask whether the interviewer has any reservations about your fit for the job; if so, attempt to erase them. Then go into your interview closing mode (see Chapter 6). Gain a sense of timing and keep the door open for follow-up contact by asking three questions: *What is the next step in the hiring process? When do you expect to make a decision? May I feel free to call if I have further questions?*

Fighting back on interview exploitation

You can lose your intellectual property through abuse of the job interview.

In the so-called *performance interview* for professional and managerial jobs, candidates are required to prove themselves with projects that demonstrate on-the-job skills, problem-solving capabilities, and communications abilities.

The employer asks for a proposal of how you'd handle a company project or requests that you design a process the company can use. You're told to be ready to "defend your ideas" at the interview.

Unfortunately, sometimes the free-sample demand is incredibly time-consuming (say, 80 hours) and costly ($200 and up in materials and research). You do your best, but suppose you don't get the job. In an example of shoddy ethics, your work samples may be given to the victorious candidate, who then steals your viable creative ideas. Here are a few examples from stung readers of my newspaper and web column.

✔ **Portfolio scam:** *When applying to an advertising agency for a copywriting job, the owner asked me to leave my portfolio for review. He kept the portfolio and called on all the clients whose work was shown in the*

portfolio! Since then, I always respond to requests to leave or send my portfolio with this statement: "I need to be there to clarify the work shown. I will be glad to bring it, and we can discuss my work at your convenience."

✔ **State government rip-off:** *When I applied for a significant and highly symbolic job with my state government, I was informed I had been selected but had to go through the formality of an interview with a key aide to the governor. As requested, I took materials and a plan for approaching the job's goals to the confirmation interview. A long, official silence followed before a form letter arrived stating that a less qualified professional, to whom I was a mentor, had won the position. The victor showed me the state's plan of action: mine.*

✔ **Consulting caper:** *My husband, an expert in human resources, spent two long days interviewing in a small town with the owner of a family company and his son. He gave them an unbelievable amount of advice and information to help their meager HR program, process management, and integrated product development. All we got out of that was*

(continued)

(continued)

reimbursement for a 200-mile car trip, a bad motel, and meals. That was our first realization of how small businesses, in particular, get almost-free consulting work.

✔ **Training trickery:** *I was a candidate for a city's new training division chief. I had to spend several hours in the city's computer labs designing programs and leaving them on CDs. I knew that, with my education and experience, I had done well. Come to find out a long-term firefighter with zero training experience got the job with the city and used my materials for new employees!*

So how do you avoid abuse without taking yourself out of the running for a job you want when you're not sure about the real interview agenda? Here are two ideas:

✔ You can copyright your plan and place a valid copyright notice ©, along with the publication date and your name, on its cover as an indication of your underlying claim to ownership. For free information, contact the Copyright Office online at www.copyright.gov, or by mail at Registrar of Copyrights, Copyright Office, Library of Congress, 101 Independence Ave. SE, Washington, DC 20559.

✔ You can bluff, hoping to create a theft deterrent by slapping a copyright notice and "Confidential — Property of (Your Name)" on your plan's cover.

When you're desperate or really, really, really want the job but don't have the time, inclination, or money to respond in full measure, offer something like this:

I'm glad that you see I have the brains and talent to bring value to your company. I'm happy, too, that you have the confidence in my work to ask me to handle such a potentially important solution to your marketing challenge. With my background, I'm sure I can do an outstanding job on this assignment. But you do realize, I hope, that such an important project would require 80 to 100 hours of intensely focused work. I'd enjoy doing it, but, quite frankly, I have several other job interviews scheduled that I really can't shift around. Do you think a sample of substantially smaller scope would serve as well for your purposes?

With a statement like this, you

✔ Remind the interviewer that you're a top candidate

✔ Promise superior results

✔ Bring a reality check to a sensitive interviewer about what's being asked of you

✔ Let the interviewer know others are interested in you

✔ Propose to do much less work until a job offer crosses your palm

You can, of course, flatly refuse to part with advance goodies. In a seller's market, you'll probably be considered anyway. But in a buyer's market, the likelihood is that you'll be passed over when you decline to turn in a hefty free sample.

Chapter 2

Getting Past Screening Interviews

In This Chapter

▶ Discovering what screening interviews are all about

▶ Preparing yourself for questions that are likely to come up

▶ Handling phone and computer screens successfully

*N*ot understanding how screening practices work in today's recruiting industry is keeping many good people on the sidelines when jobs are handed out.

Under the watchful eye of James M. Lemke, this guidebook's technical adviser and headliner in the human resource trenches, this chapter gives you the fundamentals of modern screening practices to help you survive being "screened out."

The Scoop on Screening Interviews

Screening interviews are the first step in choosing someone for a job. Designed to narrow the candidate pool for the managers who make the hiring decisions, screening interviews weed out unqualified candidates. If you don't get past this step, you're out of the running for a *selection interview* (which provides a wider and deeper evaluation of qualified candidates who survive screening interviews).

A screening interview is typically conducted by an employee in the employer's human resources department (often a support person or a junior recruiter) or by an outside recruiting contractor. Screeners can't hire you, but they can keep you from being hired.

Your goal in a screening interview is to show that your qualifications fill the employer's bill. It's not to quiz the interviewer about job suitability for factors important to you, but to keep yourself in the running for the job. So go all in to help the screener connect the dots from the job to you.

Surveying Some Common Screening Questions

Screeners usually aren't concerned with evaluating your personality or thought processes. They have one basic responsibility before putting you on an approved list and waving you up to the next interviewing level: to be sure you qualify. They do so by zeroing in on your experience, education, job-related skills, and track record.

In looking for reasons to rule you in, or to rule you out, screeners quiz you on questions that prove you can do the job — or can't do the job. Here are the kinds of job-related root questions to mentally gear up for:

- ✔ What is your experience? Can you describe your past/current day-to-day routines and duties?

- ✔ What are your skills, particularly your technical skills and competencies?

- ✔ What is your education, training, and certification?

- ✔ Where do you live? (Is your geography convenient or inconvenient? Relocations are a tough sell.)

- ✔ What is your salary requirement? (If your requirement is too low for the job's predetermined range, employers think you'll move on as soon as possible; if it's too high, they think they can't afford you.)

Additionally, screeners may send zingers your way to probe inconsistencies on your resume (such as work history gaps) or ask questions designed to highlight lies in your resume.

Presenting the Three Types of Screening Styles

Screening interviews come in three basic models:

- ✔ **Online screening questionnaire:** Questions in this model are attached to a job posting. From the company's perspective, this step is considered not an interview but a "prescreening." An organization's automated tracking system ranks a job seeker's responses based on how its recruiter weighted each question. For instance, if 100 people respond to a job posting, only the highest-ranked job seekers would be considered viable for further consideration. The next step is usually a phone screen, either automated or human.

- ✔ **Automated phone screening options:** A phoned set of preset questions is asked of all comers. Answers are recorded and often shared among company hiring managers.

- ✔ **Human screening:** A person asks specific job questions. Usually the interviewer follows a script and has no specific knowledge of the related position. Successful applicants are passed on to a hiring manager for the next step, a selection interview. Most screening interviews are conducted by telephone, whether mobile or tethered to land lines. These interviews aren't typically recorded.

Tell recruiters your salary history

Should you ever disclose your salary history or salary expectations before a job offer? Yes. Tell all when you're asked by third-party employment specialists — chiefly, executive recruiters and employment consultants who find people for jobs.

These professionals are specialists at their work and are paid for their time, on either a retained or contingency basis. They get paid to find good talent, so they won't let salary deter them from presenting you when your skills are a match for a job opening. Recruiters are far too busy with the matchmaking task to waste time with you if you make their work difficult. Time is money.

Being Prepared for Live Phone Screens

Because most people don't prepare for screening phone interviews as rigorously as they prepare for face-to-face meetings, the casualty fallout is heavy. The telephone "screen call" can come at any time, day or night. If surprises aren't your thing, stick to the steps I outline in the following sections.

Although mobile phones (including cell phones, smartphones, and feature phones) have become the norm in a mobile world, they still suffer from too many can-you-hear-me-now moments to be your first choice for a life-altering event like a screening interview. Generally, wired land-line phones of good quality remain the most reliable for excellent audio quality.

Stock your back-stage office with essentials

Stash one phone in a quiet room stocked with all your interview essentials. Must-haves include

- Your current resume (preferably customized to the job you're discussing)
- A list of your professional accomplishments
- Background information on the employer
- Questions about the company and position
- Outlines of brief stories that illustrate your qualifications and problem-solving abilities
- A calendar, with all scheduled commitments and open dates
- A notepad, pen, and calculator
- Water and tissues

Make phone appointments

Screeners sometimes purposely try to catch you with your guard down, hoping surprise strips away the outer layers of your preparation and hoping you'll blurb out genuine, unrehearsed thoughts and feelings. They may see unanticipated calls as useful for measuring your ability to think on your feet.

But you want to avoid giving answers from a brain frozen on standby status, right? Whenever possible, don't answer stuff on the fly when a call comes in. You won't be prepared and you won't do your best. Schedule an appointment for your phone interview. Say that you're walking out the door to a meeting across town and will call back as quickly as you can.

> *Thank you for calling. I appreciate your attention. I'm very interested in speaking with you about my qualifications. Unfortunately, this is not a good time for me — I'm headed out the door. Can I call you back in an hour or two? Or would tomorrow be better?*

If a recruiter insists on calling you back rather than the other way around, do what you would do for any other interview: Be ready early as a reminder to interview as a professional. Change out of your jeans and into the type of dress you'd wear in a business meeting. Most importantly, treat the call as an overture to an in-room meeting that you're going to snag by doing an excellent job on your screener.

Project your winning image

When the call comes, heed the following suggestions, most of which come from Mark S. James, a leading executive career coach (www.hireconsultant.com):

- ✔ **If you have a home office, use it.** An office just feels more businesslike. You may find it helpful to face a blank wall, to eliminate distractions of gazing out a window or spotting dust on your favorite painting.

- ✔ **Gather essential information.** At the start of the conversation, get the caller's name, title, company, e-mail address, and phone number. Read back the spelling.

- ✔ **Market yourself.** Assume the role of "seller" during the interview. If you sell your skills and abilities effectively, the listener sees value in bringing you in for an interview.

- ✔ **Strike the right tone.** Be enthusiastic, but don't dominate the conversation.

✔ **Have an answer ready.** Be prepared to answer the "tell me about yourself" request early on; keep your answer to two minutes. (You find strategic techniques for handling this key question in Chapter 4.)

✔ **Don't rush or drone on.** Speak clearly and be aware of your pace — not too fast, not too slow. Don't ramble. Keep your answers short and succinct; if the interviewer wants more information, she'll ask for it.

✔ **Use check-back phrases.** After answering a question, you can add such follow-on phrases as, *Does that answer your question? Have I sufficiently answered your question about my managerial experience? Is this the kind of information you're seeking?*

✔ **Be a champion listener.** Prove that you're paying attention by feeding back what the interviewer says: *In other words, you feel that. . . .* Interject short responses intermittently to acknowledge the interviewer's comments: *That's interesting . . . I see . . . great idea.*

✔ **Get specific.** Describe your ability to benefit the company by using specific dollar amounts and percentages to explain your past accomplishments. Let them know *how* you did it.

✔ **Divert important questions.** Tickle interviewers' interest by answering most of their questions. Then when they ask a particularly important question, give them a reason to see you in person. Tell the interviewer that you can better answer that question in person:

That's an important question — with my skills (experience) in this area, it's one that I feel I can't answer adequately over the phone. Can we set up a meeting so that I can better explain my qualifications? I'm free on Tuesday morning — is that a good time for you?

Decide beforehand which questions can best be put off for an in-person interview. You can use this tactic two or three times in the same screening conversation.

✔ **Punt the salary question.** Phone screeners often ask you to name an expected salary. Play dodge ball on this one. You don't know how much money you want yet because you don't know what the job is worth.

✔ **Push for a meeting.** As the call winds to a close, go for the prize:

As we talk, I'm thinking we can better discuss my qualifications for (position title) in person. I can be at your office Thursday morning. Is 9:30 good, or is there a better time for you?

Another statement:

(Interviewer's name), based on the information you have given me, I am very interested in pursuing this work opportunity and would like to schedule a time for us to meet in person. What looks good for you?

When the interviewer agrees but can't set a specific time, simply suggest when you're available and ask when would be a good time to follow up. Remember, what you want is an in-person meeting. Assume you'll get it and give the interviewer a choice as to the time.

✔ **Say thanks.** Express your appreciation for the time spent with you.

✔ **Write a thank-you letter.** Just because the interview was via phone doesn't negate the wisdom of putting your thanks in an e-mail.

Make your thank-you letter a sales letter that restates the qualifications you bring to the position.

Acing Automated Phone Screens

An automated screening interview in which you use a phone to answer a fixed list of questions posed by a faceless recorded voice is becoming ever more common. How successful is the technology? The answer depends on who you ask.

✔ Recruiting professionals say they like automated phone screening because they don't have to play phone tag with candidates, they can schedule blocks of time to listen to all the interviews one after another and forward the best to hiring managers, and they can listen at any hour of the day or night.

Phone interviewing when you're at work

When your current employer doesn't know that you're looking for a new job, close the door and speak to the interviewer for only a couple of minutes. Ask the caller if you can set up an in-person interview right then — or if you can talk in the evening when you're at home.

✔ Interviewees say they don't like automated phone screening because answering canned questions is cold, rigid, and impersonal. They find it uncomfortable to realize that their recorded performances can live on and on and on. They much prefer live, reactive, and unscripted responses by someone on the other end of a phone call.

Particulars vary among automated interview vendors, but here's a typical routine: For each position to be filled, the recruiter records up to 12 interview questions. Each question allows a maximum of a two-minute answer.

Automated phone screening systems often work on a "one-and-done" rule. That is, after you've recorded your answer to a question, you can't rerecord your answer even if you immediately realize that your original answer was weak or wrong. Double-check your understanding of whether the one-and-done rule applies to your interview before you begin recording.

How do you know when you're selected to interview by recording? An employer sends an interview invitation to you by e-mail or includes an "interview now" button in a website job posting.

Anticipating sticky screening questions

Be sure you're well rehearsed for potential knock-out questions that may come by phone or computer:

✔ Are you willing to relocate at your own expense?

✔ Do you have reliable transportation?

✔ Did you graduate from an accredited college?

✔ Do you have reliable child care arrangements?

✔ Would you consider a commute of more than 25 miles?

✔ Are you willing to travel 50 percent of your workweek?

Screening may also include integrity testing. Employers want to know whether you'll steal from them or otherwise turn in an ethically challenged performance. The key here? Avoid absolutes, like *always* or *never*. Recruiters aren't going to believe that you've never lied, even a teensy, tiny white lie. Find out more by browsing online for "integrity testing for employment."

To find out more about how to survive an automated phone screener, visit vendor websites. For the names of specific companies providing this type of screener, type "automated phone job interviews" into your preferred Internet search engine.

Pushing the Right Buttons: Computer Screens

Questionnaires and phone screens aren't the only screening game shows in town. Computer-assisted screens are still around, substituting meetings with a PC or app that takes you directly to a screening website, especially for jobs with high turnover, such as food service and retail. Here's what you can expect keyboard style:

- ✔ Most computer programs frame questions in a true/false or multiple-choice format, but some ask for an essay response.

- ✔ A preset time limit for each question is the norm for digital digging, so be ready to keyboard your answers in a timely manner.

Encourage a friend to try a computer interview you plan to take so you can look at the questions before diving in. Make notes of the questions and reflect on your own upcoming responses before you hit the keyboard.

Additionally, if you've never participated in a computer-controlled interview, practice on the employers you least want to work for and save the best for last, when you know what you're doing.

After you run through your computer lines, the computer compiles a summary of your answers, which the interviewer uses to decide whether you flunk the first cut or advance to the next round of interviewing.

Newer computer software allows candidates to type in comments they want to have considered — eagerness to enter or reenter the workplace, a history of unemployment due to a sick but now recovered family member, an emphasis that you're no stranger to hard work or that you never leave home without enthusiasm. Inject any comment you would have said to a human interviewer.

Handling salary boxes in online applications

Recently I was asked for a practical way to handle the *salary requirement* and *salary history* (two different things) questions when either or both are embedded as required fields in an online application. B.I. (before Internet), you could write "Negotiable" for salary expectation, to keep from under- or overpricing yourself. But most online applications won't accept "Negotiable" (or "Open" or "Will discuss in an interview") for expected salary as a viable answer, so that tactic is out history's window. What now?

To the rescue is Jack Chapman (www.salarynegotiations. com), salary consultant extraordinaire, workshop leader, and author of the best-selling guide *Negotiating Your Salary: How to Make $1,000 a Minute* (Mount Vernon Press, 2011), my favorite book in the genre. Here's what Chapman told me about working those windows:

Your self-interest is best served by putting whatever number in the salary-requirement box that you think won't get you screened out. The employer is essentially asking, "Can we afford you?" Since you won't require anything other than a competitive salary, your answer, by putting in a competitive number, is "Yes, you can afford me."

This strategy works nicely when the box is titled "Salary Requirements" or "Expected Salary," but requires an additional step if it is labeled "Current Salary." Once you're in the interview, you'll need to explain that you interpreted "Current Salary" to mean "Current Salary Requirements," and if they want a "Salary History," you'll be glad to provide it later as needed.

Chapter 3

Surveying the Many Styles of Interviews

* *

In This Chapter

▶ Discovering fresh ways to shine in any type of interview

▶ Avoiding common mistakes that can sink your chances

* *

*T*oday's job market boasts a sometimes puzzling and varied interviewing scene. Do yourself a favor and become familiar with the various shapes, forms, and fashions of interviews. You can start by checking out this chapter, which gives you the lowdown on the most common styles of job interviews. For convenience, I divide them into clusters describing the

✔ **Interviewer number,** from one to dozens

✔ **Technique and interview forms** that shape your participation

✔ **Location** where the interview takes place

Mastering Interviews by Interviewer

The most common interview style you'll encounter is the one in which a solo interviewer meets and questions you. Another possibility is that you meet face to face with several pairs of measuring eyes — all at once. Still another format shuffles you from one interview to another to another, all with the same company. I sketch the possibilities in the following sections.

One-to-one interview

You and the employer meet, usually at the employer's office, and discuss the job and your relevant skills and other qualifications that relate to it. You find suggestions on how to take victory laps in the one-to-one interview format throughout this book.

Group interview

Also called a panel, board, team, collective, or committee interview, the group interview puts you center stage before a comparatively huge crowd — perhaps 5 to 12 questioners. Usually they're people from the department where you would work, but they may come from various departments throughout the organization.

Group interviews highlight your interpersonal skills, leadership, and ability to think on your feet and deal with issues in a stressful setting. The purpose of a group interview is not only to hear what you say but also to see what behaviors and skills you display within a group.

You wouldn't be at this expensive meeting (think of all the salaries for the group's time) if you hadn't already been screened to be sure your qualifications are acceptable. These people are gathered to see whether they like you and whether you'll fit into their operation. Greet each person, handing out a fresh copy of your resume. Appear confident. Make a quick seating chart to help you remember names.

Before you answer the first question, smile, thank everyone for inviting you to meet with them, and then begin your answer, which will probably be "You asked me to tell you about myself. . . ."

 Should you try to identify the leader and direct most of your remarks to that person? Not necessarily. The boss may be the quiet observer in the corner. Play it safe — maintain eye contact with all committee members.

 Ask questions. Periodically summarize important points to keep the group focused. Use a notebook to record several simultaneous questions, explaining that you don't want to omit responding to anyone's important concern.

When the interview is over, thank the group as though you just finished a speech.

> *Thank you for having me here today. I enjoyed being with you. This interview confirmed my research indicating that this company is a good place to work. I'll look forward to hearing from you and, hopefully, joining you.*

Serial interview

A serial interview also involves a group of people, but not all at once. You're handed off from person to person, typically from screener to line manager to top manager — and perhaps a half-dozen people in between. You strengthen your chances each time you're passed onward.

Use your screening (plain vanilla personality) interview behavior with all interviewers you meet except those with whom you would work. Then go into your selection (full personality) mode.

When the initial interviewer says that you're being passed on to the second interviewer, try to find out a little about the second interviewer. Ask a question like "Does number two feel the same way about customer service as you do?" This way you'll get information you need to establish common ground with your next interviewer. Continue the advance-tip technique all the way to the finish line.

When you're interviewed by one person after another, consistency counts. Don't tell a rainbow of stories about the same black-and-white topics. When interview team members later compare notes, they should be discussing the same person.

Mastering Interviews by Technique

A job interviewer sets the technique and tone of the interview, whether it's behavior based, tightly or loosely controlled, intentionally stressful, or loaded with brain-crunching puzzles.

Brainteaser job interview

If you were to eliminate one of the 50 United States, leaving only 49 states, which one would it be and why?

That's a question Microsoft interviewers like to ask, says John Kador, business writing consultant (www.jkador.com) and author of a smart book on logic-driven riddles and oxygen-sucking puzzles that job interviewers may spring on you without warning.

Brainteasers ("Why are manhole covers round?" or "How would you test a salt shaker?") ordinarily are reserved for very bright candidates as a challenge to see who can rise and shine in professional and managerial positions in today's hypercompetitive work environment.

When you suspect that you're heading into interview combat, find guidance in Kador's book, *How to Ace the Brain Teaser Interview* (McGraw-Hill).

So what's the best answer if you're smacked upside the head with that Microsoft state-elimination haymaker? "Well, it's *not* the state of Washington," Kador says with a grin. (Microsoft is headquartered in Redmond, Washington.)

Behavior-based interview

Behavior-based interviewing relies on storytelling — examples of what you've done that support your claims. Premised on the belief that the past predicts the future, behavior-based interviewing techniques are used to ask candidates how they've handled specific situations — what kinds of behaviors they used to solve problems.

The presumption is that if you were a good problem solver in the past, you'll be a good problem solver in the future. Behavior-based interviewing emphasizes "What did you do when?" rather than "What would you do if?"

Behavior-based interview questions are designed to draw out clues to a candidate's workplace DNA. All candidates are asked virtually the same questions. The tip-off that you've just been handed a behavior-based question, which should be answered with a demonstrated skill or trait, is when the question begins with words such as these:

- ✔ Tell me about a time when —
- ✔ Give me an example of your skills in —
- ✔ Describe a time when you —
- ✔ Why did you —

A few fleshed-out examples illustrate the behavior-based technique more fully:

> *Think back to a time when you were on the verge of making a huge sale, and the customer balked at the last minute, promised to get back to you, but didn't. What action did you take?*

> *Remember a time when you improved inventory turns; how big of an improvement did you make?*

> *Tell me about an on-the-job disaster that you turned around, making lemonade from lemons.*

> *Describe the types of risks you have allowed your direct reports to take.*

> *Can you give me an example of when you were able to implement a vision for your organization?*

> *Why did you decide to major in sociology at San Marcos State University instead of at a small private college?*

Companies using behavior-based interviewing first must identify the behaviors important to the job. If leadership, for instance, is one of the valued behaviors, several questions asking for stories of demonstrated leadership will be asked:

> *Tell me about the last time you had to take charge of a project but were lacking in clear direction. How did you carry forward the project?*

In mining your past for anecdotes, you can draw from virtually any part of your past behavior — education, paid work experience, volunteer work, activities, hobbies, family life.

As you sift through your memories, be on the lookout for a theme, the motif that runs through your choices of education, jobs, and activities. Put at least half a dozen anecdotes that illustrate your theme in your mental pocket and pull them out when you need them. Examples of themes are as follows:

✔ Displaying leadership

✔ Solving problems

✔ Negotiating

✔ Showing initiative

✔ Overcoming adversity

✔ Succeeding

✔ Dealing with stress

✔ Sacrificing to achieve an important work goal

✔ Dealing with someone who disagrees with you

✔ Displaying commitment

✔ Demonstrating work ethic

✔ Staying task orientated

✔ Practicing communication skills

Here are several more suggestions to tap-dance your way through behavior-based questions:

✔ Tell a story with a beginning, a middle, and an end using the PAR technique — problem, action, result.

Here's an example: *Problem:* An e-commerce company was operating at a substantial loss. *Action:* I outsourced technical support and added seven new product lines. *Result:* We cut our expenses by 8 percent, increased our revenues by 14 percent, and had our first profitable year, with expectations of higher profits next year.

✔ Try not to sound as though you memorized every sylla-ble and inflection, or like a machine with all the answers. Admitting that your example was a complex problem and that you experimented until you found its best solution humanizes you.

Realize that the behavior-based interviewer is more interested in the process than in the details of your success stories. What was the reasoning behind your actions? Why did you behave the way you did? What skills did you use?

Directive interview

The *directive interview* is one in which the interviewer maintains complete control and walks you through the discussion to uncover what he or she wants to know.

The *structured* interview is directive because the interviewer works from a written list of questions asked of all candidates and writes down your answers.

The argument in favor of structured interviews is that they promote fairness, uncover superior candidates, and eliminate the cloning effect (in which an interviewer essentially hires candidates in his own image — or one who the interviewer thinks will "fit in" merely because of shared values).

In structured interviews, the interviewer may throw out a critical incident and ask you to respond. A *critical incident* is a specific problem or challenge that was successfully handled by employees of the company. Like a quiz show, the host (the interviewer) has the "answer sheet" — the actual behavior that solved the problem or met the challenge.

 Some critical incidents can be anticipated by researching industry trends and inferred by reading company press releases online.

Whether you're in an unwritten directive interview or a scripted structured interview, expect interviewers to ask both closed- and open-ended questions.

- ✔ **A closed-ended question** can be answered with *yes* or *no*: Did you find my office easily?

- ✔ **An open-ended question** usually asks *how* or *why*: How do you like this industry?

The directive interviewer has an agenda and is intent on seeing that it's followed. Being too assertive in changing the topic is a mistake. The only safe way you can introduce one of your skills is to ask a question, such as "Would you like to hear about my experience in quality assessment?"

Nondirective interview

A *nondirective interview* rewards you for leading the discussion. It's often an approach of line managers who don't know much about professional interviewing.

Questions tend to be broad and general so that you can elaborate and tell all kinds of terrific stories about yourself. A few questions may reveal key areas of the employer's needs. These questions may sound at first as though they're critical incidents, but in this loose-limbed interview, the interviewer probably doesn't assume that he or she knows the answers. Examples of nondirective interview questions include the following:

> *We had a problem employee last quarter who revealed information about our marketing strategies to a competitor — how would you handle this situation?*
>
> *You understand some of the difficulties this department faces — how would you approach these in your first four months?*
>
> *Tell me about your goals in the next five years and how this position fits in with them.*
>
> *Your resume shows you have a degree in Spanish and another in computer science — how do you plan to use both of these in this position?*

Carry agenda cards or a small notebook with a list of your qualifications and a list of questions about the company. When you have to carry the ball, working from notes can be a lifesaver if you have a leaky memory.

If all your preparation fails you, fall back on "I wish I had the answer. What's your viewpoint on this?"

Stress interview

Recognizing the hazing that goes on in a stress interview is important; recognize it for what it is — either it's a genuine test of your ability to do the job, or you're being punk'd by a certified jerk.

Suppose, for example, that you're in sales. Asking you to sell the interviewer something — like the office chair — is fairly common. But having you face blinding sunlight while sitting in a chair with one short leg is, at best, immature.

Stress interviews often consist of

- ✔ Hour-long waits before the interview
- ✔ Long, uncomfortable silences
- ✔ Challenges of your beliefs
- ✔ A brusque interviewer or multiple curt interviewers
- ✔ Deliberate misinterpretation of your comments and outright insults

Typical questions run along these lines:

Why weren't you working for so long?

Why eight jobs in ten years?

Your resume shows that you were with your last company for a number of years without promotion and a virtually flat salary; why is that?

Can you describe a situation when your work was criticized or you disliked your boss?

Would you like to have my job?

What would you do if violence erupted in your workplace?

Never take the horrors of a stress interview personally. Keep your cool and play the game if you want the job. Don't sweat. Don't cry. Your most reliable tactic is to speak with calm, unflagging confidence. You may have to practice remaining poised in the face of an interviewer's intimidation tactics.

A famous admiral, now dead, used to nail the furniture to the floor and ask the applicant to pull up a chair. If an interviewer crosses your personal line of reasonable business behavior, stand up with dignity, thank the interviewer for the time, and run like hell for the emergency exit.

Bravo moves for all interviewing styles

No matter what style of interview you're participating in, some factors are all-purpose job winners.

✔ **Make them like you.** No matter how scientific the interviewing style, the quality of likeability is a powerful influence in deciding who gets the job. And it's human nature to like people who like us, and who are like us in common interests and outlooks.

Show your similarities to the interviewer and company culture. You need not be clones of each other, but do find areas of mutual interest: preferences in movies, methods of doing work, or favorite company products, for instance. When you successfully intimate that you and the decision-making interviewer share similar worldviews, values, or approaches to work, you create affinity that leads to job offers.

✔ **Listen well to interviewers' questions, statements, and feelings.** People like to be listened to more than they like to listen. Show your likeability by summarizing, rephrasing, and playing back what interviewers say instead of concentrating just on what you have to say.

✔ **Don't overdo the compliments or small talk.** Take cues from the interviewer's office mementos just long enough to break the ice. Most interviewers will be turned off by such transparent plays for empty approval. Get to the point — the job.

✔ **Pause thoughtfully.** Show that you think as you talk. It's okay to pause in thoughtfulness during an in-person interview, where interviewers can tell you're contemplating and thinking things through before answering. *Exception:* Don't take a thinking pause in a telephone or video-conferencing interview, where any pause is dead airtime.

✔ **Take notes.** Have a small note-book handy and use it when the interviewer is talking, especially after you've asked a question or the interviewer has put special emphasis on a subject. Taking notes shows that you're paying attention *and* it flatters the interviewer. If you prefer to use a laptop or tablet to take notes, ask first: "May I make a few notes as we talk? I don't want to forget any of your key points."

Mastering Interviews at Remote Locations

Not every interview takes place across a desk at the company's home base. You may have to interview over a meal or at a job fair. I help you conquer these interviewing challenges in the next sections.

Mealtime interview

Just when you thought you'd been through all the interviewing hoops and assumed that landing the job was a done deal, you get a luncheon invitation from a higher-up in the company, perhaps your potential boss. Why? Robin Jay, author of *The Art of the Business Lunch: Building Relationships Between 12 and 2* (Career Press), identifies the following reasons:

- ✔ To judge you on your social skills and manners
- ✔ To find out additional information about you that an employer may not legally be able to ask
- ✔ To get to know you better
- ✔ To compare your social behavior to that of other candidates

As an account executive, Jay ate her way through 3,000 business lunches. (No, she's not fat.) She says that sharing a meal with someone reveals her personality faster and more effectively than all the office interviews in the world. "Many a job has been won or lost at the table," Jay observes.

Although a mealtime interview may seem more relaxed and social, stay as alert as you would in any other location. Mealtime interviewers are watching you with big eyes, so keep the following in mind to avoid spilling precious job opportunities:

- ✔ Don't order entrees so hard to eat that you spend the entire interview lost in your plate with long pasta or saucy, messy, or bony food.
- ✔ Don't order alcohol unless you're at dinner — even then, have only one drink. White wine is a good choice.

✔ Don't order the most expensive or the most inexpensive thing on the menu.

✔ Don't smoke (companies are obsessed with employee health costs).

✔ Don't complain about anything — the food, the service, or the restaurant.

✔ Don't over-order or leave too much food on your plate.

To look classy in a mealtime interview, be sure to

✔ Order something that's either easy to eat, like a club or veggie sandwich, or similar to what the interviewer orders. (Alternatively, you can always ask what the interviewer recommends.)

✔ Chew with your mouth closed and speak with your mouth empty.

✔ Show your appreciation for the treat — once hired, you may find yourself brown-bagging your lunch.

Cool tool: The branding brief

Kathryn Kraemer Troutman, executive career consultant and CEO of The Resume Place, Inc., (www.resume-place.com) in Baltimore, recommends that job seekers devise an abbreviated personal marketing message, one that she terms a *branding brief.* The length of a branding brief is 20 to 30 seconds, or about 100 words.

A similar synopsis may also be called a *mini-elevator speech,* a *personal branding message,* or a *profile summary;* all these terms refer to a capsule of your "story" as it relates to an employer.

Consider incorporating a branding brief within your one- to two-minute personal commercial for interviews, use it as a standalone statement in networking, or leave it behind after a job interview. A branding brief has more "sell" than a factual short bio and is presented in a less formal style.

A branding brief headlines what you are known for. It identifies your special characteristics and achievements of interest to an employer. You can use a branding brief to help people remember who you are, why you're memorable, and when they should seek you, Troutman explains.

"In constructing a branding brief, describe your top characteristics and how they can contribute to the mission of an organization that you hope to join. Clearly state how you can help achieve the organization's mission." Here are a few of Troutman's branding brief content examples:

✔ *As a kid, I listened to old radio programs that said things like, "The Shadow Knows. . . ." Right then, I developed a life-long passion for radio. In a complex media marketplace, you can count on me as a proven programming manager to target and deliver larger audiences.*

I offer expert marketing and distribution skills that I'll stack up against anyone's in the business. As a programming chief, I've got the whole package of skills, from affiliate contract negotiation and content, to audience and technology. In short, I hope you'll agree that I know more about leading a programming effort than the Shadow ever knew . . . although the Shadow knew a lot!

✔ *My name is Keri Bright, and I formerly taught English at Martingale High School, where I was known for establishing community literacy programs to teach immigrants how to read and write English. My bilingual*

skills would be useful as an aide in the Congressman's office.

✔ *I successfully worked as a library technician in the James River Free Library, with diverse accomplishments ranging from multimedia productions and program development, to speaker recruitment and publication selection for special markets.*

After getting real library experience for six years, I invested in a library science degree program to upgrade my professional competencies and skills. Now I'm ready to begin work on blending technology, archives, and library services in efficient and affordable programs to excite library patrons.

✔ *My career as a logistics specialist — some people call that supply-chain specialist — is very rewarding, as I work to see that important materials and resources get to the right place at the right time for the right price. I'm a perfect fit for your position, where I would continue working my magic for your customers — managing inventory, distributing goods, and monitoring the quality of materials provided.*

A mealtime interview is the perfect occasion to practice a technique known as *mirroring* — what the boss or the interviewer does, you do. Take the interviewer's lead in where to rest arms on the table, which fork to hold, and how fast to shovel in the food. Subconsciously, you're establishing similarities, making the interviewer like you.

Always be polite to the food server, even if the service or food is so bad you make a mental note never to set foot in the place again. Treating the server with disrespect is worse than spilling spaghetti sauce all over the interviewer's new suit.

No matter how much or how little the tab, the interviewer always pays, so don't reach for the bill when it comes, even if it's placed closer to you. Let it sit there unclaimed, unloved. After all, this could be a test of your confidence or of your knowledge of protocol.

Job fair interview

Job fairs are brief but significant encounters in which you hand over documents — either your resume or a summary sheet of your qualifications (carry both types of documents). Your objective is to land an interview, not get a job offer on the spot at the fair. At best, you'll get a screening interview at the event site.

Try to preregister for the job fair, get a list of participating employers, and research those you plan to visit. Your edge is to be better prepared than the competition.

Fair lines are long, so accept the likelihood that you'll be standing in many of them. Make use of your time by writing up notes from one recruiter while standing in line to meet another.

Everyone tries to arrive early, so think about arriving at half-time when the first flood has subsided. Dress professionally, whatever that means in your career field.

Work up a branding brief with at least one strong memorable point to say to recruiters. (I tell you all about branding briefs in the nearby sidebar.) If there's no immediate feedback inviting you for an interview, hand over your summary sheet and ask, "Do you have positions appropriate for my background?" If the answer is positive, your next question is "I'd like to take the next step — can we set up an interview?" If you don't get a positive response, continue with "Can we talk on the phone next week?"

Whether or not you're able to schedule an interview on the spot, when you leave, hand over your resume.

Chapter 4

Answering Questions with Ease

- -

In This Chapter

▶ Presenting the best you in the face of any question

▶ Checking out some winning — and some downright awful — responses

▶ Knowing when a question crosses into illegal or inappropriate territory

- -

*Q*uestions are the beginning, middle, and end of any interview story. How you respond to them is one of the primary ways interviewers get a feel for who you are and what you can do.

This chapter runs down the do's and don'ts of answering questions about yourself, your skills, and your expected salary. It fills you in on responding to questions about the job you hope is ahead and the jobs you've had in the past. It also covers questions about hard-to-market situations and tells you how to handle sticky questions you may not want to answer.

 After the interviewing Q&A begins, what should you do if you don't understand one of the questions? Ask for clarification. Say something like, "I'm not sure I understand your question, and I don't want to give you an irrelevant or incorrect answer."

Telling Someone about Yourself

In trying to figure out whether you're the right person to hire, interviewers usually start with the parent of self-revealing questions, often phrased as a statement:

Tell me a little about yourself.

No matter how the question is worded, take care to get your act together for it, because it comes early in an interview — at the very time when an interviewer is forming an initial impression of you.

Employers want to know how well you accept management direction. They want to know whether you have a history of slacking off as you get too comfortable on a job. They want to know whether — despite their lack of long-term commitment to you — you'll jump ship at an inconvenient time if another employer dangles more money before your eyes.

When answering the Tell Me About Yourself question, bear the following thought in mind:

Focus on the Best You.

Always be honest about the wonderful parts of you. But don't wildly exaggerate your best traits to the extent that your performance bears no relationship to your promise. Remember that the piper who lives down the road will demand to be paid — possibly at a very inconvenient time.

You can jump right in and answer the Tell Me About Yourself question, or you can ask for prompts:

I can tell you about experience and accomplishments in this industry, or the education and training that qualify me for this position, or about my personal history. Where shall I start?

Employers typically answer that they want to hear about both your work and relevant background — or a little bit of everything.

In addition to the Tell Me About Yourself question, you may be asked any of the following questions. ShowStoppers are answers that work for you; Clunkers and Bloopers are answers that work against you.

What is your most memorable accomplishment?

ShowStoppers

> ✔ Relate an accomplishment directly to the job for which you're interviewing.
>
> ✔ Give details about the accomplishment, as if you're telling a story.
>
> ✔ Describe the problem, the action you took, and the results (known as the PAR technique).

Clunkers and Bloopers

> ✔ Give a vague or unfocused answer.
>
> ✔ Talk about an accomplishment with no connection to the job you want.
>
> ✔ Discuss responsibilities rather than results.

Where do you see yourself five years from now? How does this position fit with your long-term career objectives?

ShowStoppers

> ✔ Say you hope your hard work has moved you appropriately forward on your career track.
>
> ✔ Answer realistically: In a changed business world where a long-term job may mean three years, speak of lifelong education to keep abreast of changes in your field and self-reliance for your own career.
>
> ✔ Describe short-term, achievable goals and discuss how they'll help you reach your long-term goals.
>
> ✔ Explain how the position you're interviewing for will help you reach your goals.
>
> ✔ Strive to look ambitious, but not so much so that the hiring manager feels threatened.

Clunkers and Bloopers

- ✔ Say that you want the interviewer's job.
- ✔ Describe unrealistic goals.
- ✔ Flippantly say that you expect to see yourself in mirrors and on YouTube.
- ✔ State goals the company doesn't need or can't satisfy.

What is your greatest strength?

ShowStoppers

- ✔ Anticipate and prepare to discuss up to five strengths, such as
  - Skill in managing your work schedule
  - Willingness to do extra
  - Ability to learn quickly
  - Proficiency at solving problems
  - Team-building skills
  - Leadership skills
  - Cool, analytical temperament under pressure
- ✔ Discuss only strengths related to the position you want.
- ✔ Use specific examples to illustrate. Include statistics and testimonials.

Clunkers and Bloopers

- ✔ Discuss strengths unrelated to the job you want.
- ✔ Fumble around, saying that you don't feel comfortable bragging about yourself.
- ✔ Sell yourself too hard without delivering tangible evidence to back up your claims.
- ✔ For women only: Bring up the fact that you're president of your child's PTA (unless you're interviewing for a job selling school supplies). Discriminatory? Yes, but studies show that moms may be seen as less committed to jobs than either childless women or men (with or without kids).

What is your greatest weakness?

ShowStoppers

✔ Explain that because of the corrective action you took, you were able to transform a starting point of failure into a success story of strength. Four examples follow:

- *Not being a natural techie, I was underperforming when I first worked with X word-processing software. So I took a class in that program at a community college on my own time, and now I'm the best administrative assistant in my office.*

- *I didn't always know what I was doing — right or wrong — when I took my first managerial position. So I took online classes in managerial techniques, read management books, and paid attention to how managers whom I admired operated. As a result, I give careful thought to the quality of guidance that I give my direct reports before launching a project. I'm not yet perfect and may never be — I'm my own toughest critic — but, as the record shows, my leadership has improved dramatically in motivating the productivity achievements of my teams.*

- *I've had trouble remembering the timing of every appointment when I had to move like lightning across town from one sales call to another sales call. But I've corrected that scheduling problem with this terrific smartphone. I haven't missed a call since I got it.*

- *I'm determined to complete whatever I start, and occasionally I can see myself getting hard-headed about it. But then I step back and recall the difference between completing a project and committing an act of stubbornness and make a course correction. Shall I tell you about the time when I —?*

✔ Cite a shortcoming you're working on, even if you haven't completely turned the weakness around — yet. Three examples follow:

- *I'm working on my time-management skills, quickly learning not to take on an overload of work if it threatens the quality of my work products. For example, I now write to-do lists and assign priorities.*

- *I'm working on cooling my tendency to be impatient. It's my nature to want to accomplish things as fast and efficiently as possible, and when others stall my progress, I lose patience. I remind myself every morning that others are busy people, too. Now I cut co-workers more slack on getting back to me before I send a friendly reminder.*

- *English is my second language. But I'm taking a class and listening to speech on TV, and my language ability is getting better every day.*

✔ Balance a weakness with a compensating strength. Three examples follow:

- *I'm not a global thinker. But being detail minded, I'm a top-notch staffer to an executive who is a big-picture guy.*

- *I don't pretend to be a gifted trial lawyer. But I'll stack my legal research and business structure skills up against any other lawyer in town.*

- *As a newcomer to this city, I can't bring a clientele to this job, but I can use my talent for public presentations to build one faster than you can say "Give me a quote." I have a plan to attract clients by quickly becoming known as a speaker at local club meetings and civic events.*

✔ Choose a weakness that doesn't matter to the job's success. An example follows:

- *I'm a very organized person, but you'd never know it by looking at my desk, which sometimes qualifies for the cover of Better Landfills magazine.*

✔ Rhetorically rephrase the question aloud to make your shortcoming seem less of a minus. One example follows:

- *Let me think . . . what attributes, when improved, would make me perform even better in this job? Hmm. . . . Then identify areas in which you want more training or guidance.*

Clunkers and Bloopers

✔ Mention a brutally honest negative, such as you're hard to work with, you're easily bored, you're lazy, you don't get along well with minority co-workers, you have a poor memory or a hot temper, or you're exhausted by stress.

✔ Fall back on clichés. Examples: You're a workaholic. *(My boss has to shove me out the door every night to make me go home.)* You're a perfectionist. *(The devil is in the time-eating details, and I sweat every one.)*

✔ Say you have no weaknesses.

✔ Volunteer key weaknesses that were likely to go unnoticed in the hiring decision.

Would you rather work with others or alone? How about teams?

ShowStoppers

✔ Discuss your adaptability and flexibility in working with others as a leader or a follower. At heart, you're always a team player, but in certain situations, you prefer to work alone.

✔ Give concrete examples.

✔ Mention the importance of every team member's contribution.

Clunkers and Bloopers

✔ Appear to be overly dependent on a team to see you through.

✔ Let the interviewer think that you're a pushover, willing to carry the load of team members who don't contribute.

✔ Say you don't like to work on teams.

What is your definition of success? Of failure?

ShowStoppers

✔ Show that your success is balanced between your professional and personal lives.

✔ Relate success to the position you want.

✔ If you have to talk about failure, do so positively. Show how you turned a failure into a success, or discuss how and what you learned from the failure.

✔ Demonstrate that you're a happy person who thinks the world is more good than bad.

Clunkers and Bloopers

✔ Spend a great deal of time talking about failure.

✔ Say that you've never failed or made mistakes.

✔ Discuss success as a ruthless, take-no-prisoners shot to the top.

How do you handle stressful situations?

ShowStoppers

✔ Give examples of how you've dealt with job stress.

✔ Discuss what you do to relax, refresh, and refill.

✔ Give positive illustrations of how job stress makes you work harder or more efficiently.

Clunkers and Bloopers

✔ Say that you avoid stress. (What, me worry?)

✔ Imply that stress is usually the result of lack of preparation or knowledge.

Is there anything else I should know about you?

ShowStoppers

✔ Discuss any selling points the interview failed to uncover and relate those selling points to the job you want.

✔ Repeat the selling points you've already discussed and remind the interviewer why you're the best candidate for the job.

Clunkers and Bloopers

✔ Say "No." And not another word.

✔ Remark that you will require the first two weeks off every June for vacation because that's when your timeshare is available.

Why should I hire you?

ShowStoppers

> ✔ Prepare at least three key reasons to roll off your tongue that show how you're better than the other candidates. Use specific examples to illustrate your reasons.

> ✔ Tell something unusual or unique about you that will make the interviewer remember you.

Clunkers and Bloopers

> ✔ Dance around this question without really addressing it.

> ✔ Say you would be an asset to the company bowling team; your house payment is overdue; you need a change of scenery.

> ✔ Tell the interviewer, "You need to fill the job."

Answering Questions Related to the Job, Company, and Industry

Employers expect you to grasp what the job entails and how it fits into the overall company picture. For responsible professional jobs, they're even more impressed if you've looked into what the company does and where it stands in its industry.

Look at the following questions and the strategies you can use to answer them as you gear up to show how you're a perfect fit for your target job and the company offering it. Choose strategies marked as ShowStoppers; avoid those indicated to be Clunkers and Bloopers.

What do you know about this position?

ShowStoppers

> ✔ From your research, discuss how the position fits into the company structure and how you would fit like a glove into that position.

> ✔ Mention how you can help the company achieve its goals.

✔ Confirm your understanding of the broad responsibilities of the position. Ask whether you missed any key points (thereby setting up topics to discuss your qualifications).

Clunkers and Bloopers

✔ Ask what the company makes.

✔ Use out-of-date data.

What do you know about our competition?

ShowStoppers

✔ Discuss the current climate of the industry and how competitors are affected.

✔ Add details that show you truly understand the industry and the competition.

✔ Analyze the impact global competition is having on the industry.

Clunkers and Bloopers

✔ Say you know very little about the competition.

✔ Admit you recently interviewed with the competition.

✔ Reveal trade secrets from your current employer.

What are your opinions about some of the challenges facing our company?

ShowStoppers

✔ Show the depth of your research by discussing some of the company's upcoming projects.

✔ Mention several possible solutions to potential problems the company may be facing, acknowledging that you lack certainty without proprietary facts.

Clunkers and Bloopers

✔ Say you don't know of any challenges, but you're all ears.

✔ Mention problems but add no possible solutions.

What do you see as the direction of this company?

ShowStoppers

> ✔ Give a brief but somewhat detailed answer, displaying a solid grasp of the company's movement in the industry. Add how you can help.

> ✔ Support your answer with facts and figures, citing their sources.

Clunkers and Bloopers

> ✔ Make guesses because you haven't a clue.

> ✔ Offer no data to back up your comments.

Why did you apply to this company?

ShowStoppers

> ✔ Say that the position is a compelling opportunity and the company is a place where your qualifications can make a difference. Explain why.

> ✔ Relate that you heard about a new service the company is launching, which is somewhat related to a project you once worked on; say you find the potential exciting. Ask if the interviewer would like to hear about your project.

Clunkers and Bloopers

> ✔ State that the company is in an industry you've always wanted to try.

> ✔ Say you've always wanted to live in the Southwest (or whatever part of the country the company or position happens to be located in).

Our company has a mission statement; do you have a personal mission statement — or personal vision?

ShowStoppers

> ✔ In one or two sentences, give examples of your values (customer service, ethics, honor, importance of keeping one's word, and so on) that are compatible with the company's.

> ✔ Review the company's mission statement on its website and describe a compatible aim.

Clunkers and Bloopers

> ✔ Ask what a mission statement is.
>
> ✔ Ask for clarification on the meaning of values.

How will you help our company?

ShowStoppers

> ✔ Summarize how your key skills can help the company move toward its goals.
>
> ✔ Describe the wide circle of contacts and other intangible benefits you can bring to the company.

Clunkers and Bloopers

> ✔ Give a short answer with no specifics.
>
> ✔ Say you'll have to get back to the interviewer on that one.

Answering Questions about Your Skills

Use storytelling to comprehensively answer skills questions. Remember, too, that social, or soft, skills (people skills) play a significant role in determining the winning candidate. Take pains to convince the interviewer that you're a pleasant individual who gets along with people.

Consider this question, which is used to see how you react using such skills as conflict management and interpersonal relationships:

> *How would you deal with a difficult boss?*

Here's an answer, underscored with storytelling that makes you look like a reasonable and conscientious person:

> *I would first try to make sure that the difficulty isn't walking around in my shoes. Then I'd read a few books on how to*

interact with difficult people. I've never had a boss I didn't like, but I have had to use tact on occasion.

On my last job, my boss and I didn't see eye to eye on the best software for an office application. I researched the issue in detail and wrote a short, fact-filled report for my boss. Based on this new information, my boss then bought the software I recommended.

This answer centers on research skills but also highlights patience and acceptance of supervision.

The following sample skills questions are generalized for wider application. In an interview, you should expect skills questions that relate to your career field: *What computer skills do you have? Why do you think your technical skills are a match for this job? When is the best time to close a sale? What was your most difficult auditing problem and how did you solve it? Tell me about your typical workday as a probation officer.*

What is the toughest job problem you've ever faced?

ShowStoppers

> ✔ Recall a problem, the *skills used in your action* to deal with it, and the successful results; this is a skills-detailed version of PAR (problem, action, result).

> ✔ Explain how you can apply those same skills to the prospective job.

Clunkers and Bloopers

> ✔ Recall a problem but not an accomplishment or skill related to it.

> ✔ Say you've searched your memory and can't recall a problem you couldn't handle.

What do you like least about gathering information to deal with a problem (research)?

ShowStoppers

> ✔ Comment that, wanting to do a first-rate job, you're uncomfortable when you're uncertain that you've compiled enough research to quit and make a decision that affects the well-being of others.

✓ Reveal that you enjoy solving problems but become impatient with repetitive same-ol'-same-ol' answers leading to dead ends.

✓ Explain that you use multiple resources — websites, books, journals, and experts — and you become frustrated when key resources aren't adequate.

Clunkers and Bloopers

✓ Dismiss researching as work for the scholars among us and say you prefer to be an action hero. (Even bank robbers have to case the job.)

✓ Admit you prefer outdoor work and aren't sure why you're here.

How good are you at making oral presentations?

ShowStoppers

✓ Discuss how you prepare. Name presentation skills. Mention specific instances when you know you've performed well.

✓ Offer to give a one-minute oral presentation on a topic you've practiced.

Clunkers and Bloopers

✓ Say that you never do them because you're terrified of speaking in front of large crowds.

✓ Admit you were roundly booed at your last political protest speech.

How would you rate your writing skills in comparison to your verbal skills?

ShowStoppers

✓ Discuss how both skills — as well as listening — are important to being a good communicator and that although one or the other may be your strong suit, you're working to become strongly proficient at both speaking and writing. Explain how you're doing so — class work, independent study, membership in Toastmasters International or a writing group; show brief writing samples.

✔ Concretely explain a real communication situation in your past; describe how you communicated the information and the result.

✔ If you're a weak communicator, give a compensatory response that substitutes another skill for writing or verbal skills; for example, in a technical call center, problem solving outweighs the need for golden tonsils and laudable business writing.

Clunkers and Bloopers

✔ Rate your skill in one area as better than the other and clam up.

✔ Say that public speaking gives you sweaty palms and you don't like it.

How do you deal with unexpected events on the job?

ShowStoppers

✔ Discuss how you immediately reprioritize your assignments in emergencies.

✔ Mention specific instances when you were able to complete a project (or projects) on time despite unforeseen complications.

Clunkers and Bloopers

✔ Tell how you just keep doing what you're doing until you're finished.

✔ Discuss an instance when an unexpected event resulted in disaster.

How do you organize your time?

ShowStoppers

✔ Affirm that you put first things first. Each day you identify A-level tasks and get those done before moving on to B-level tasks. You return voicemail messages once or twice daily and urgent messages immediately.

✔ Comment that you use up-to-date planning products. These include planning software such as PlanPlusOnline and PDA (personal digital assistant) hand-held devices, such as a BlackBerry. These kinds of mentions show that you are techno-current. If you organize yourself on paper, mention a formal business product such as a Franklin Planner. (Pulling out a pocket calendar is like pulling out a slide rule.) Conclude with true examples showing that you've completed multiple tasks on time.

✔ Discuss how you went through a typical day on one of your previous jobs.

Clunkers and Bloopers

✔ Say that you don't usually handle more than one task at a time.

✔ Reply that you don't wear a watch.

How do you delegate responsibility?

ShowStoppers

✔ Discuss how you involve everyone in the overall picture.

✔ Talk about specific projects that were successful because of your team effort.

Clunkers and Bloopers

✔ Reveal that you like process detail; admit your micro-managing tendencies to tell direct reports how to connect every dot.

✔ Mention your belief that a task will be done right only if you do it yourself.

What's your experience with group projects (teamwork)?

ShowStoppers

✔ Mention a specific project, including the group goals and your particular responsibilities.

✔ Discuss your positive relationship with the project supervisor; compliment co-workers.

Clunkers and Bloopers

> ✔ Don't identify your responsibilities; just say you all worked together.
>
> ✔ Rip your co-workers as laggards and say you're sick of doing most of the heavy lifting without credit.

Why should I hire you?

ShowStoppers

> ✔ Summarize point by point why your qualifications match the employer's needs to a tee, adding any additional competitive edge you can honestly claim. (Rehearse in advance to avoid stumbles.)
>
> ✔ Include accomplishments and the skills that facilitated those accomplishments, plus relevant experience and training.

Clunkers and Bloopers

> ✔ Fail to make the "perfect match" connection.
>
> ✔ Offer only clichés, such as "I'm honest, hardworking, and a fast learner," without factual backup illustrations.

Making Your Experience Relevant

Psychologists insist that past behavior predicts future behavior. True or not, interviewers look at your yesterdays for clues as to how well you'll perform in your tomorrows.

 Simply reciting your experience isn't going to excite an employer. You have to make the connection between then and now. You must show exactly how your experience-based accomplishments make you the perfect candidate for the job opening. Here's a straightforward example:

> *As you'll note on my resume, I've had five years of praised experience as an instructor and training coordinator. I'd like to tell you a few details about my work as an office-work*

> *trainer for military spouses, which has a direct application to your project to retrain a portion of the company's plant workers. Would you like to hear a bit about that?*

Whether you have a lot or a little experience, employers want to hire people who will continue to learn and grow to the benefit of their company. So as you answer the experience questions, focus not only on your experience but also on how your efforts served the changing needs of your previous employer. Case in point:

> *I started training the military wives on word-processing programs from 9 a.m. until noon three days a week. After several months, I was asked to add evening hours two nights a week to train a class on spreadsheet programs, which I myself had to quickly get up to steam on — and was glad to do so.*

When you can show how you've successfully adapted in the past, convincing employers that you have what it takes to adapt your experience to their workplaces is easier.

Following are examples of questions that you may be asked about your work experience, along with suggested answering techniques (ShowStoppers) and definite mistakes (Clunkers and Bloopers).

What kind of experience do you have for this job?

ShowStoppers

- ✔ Gather information before answering. Ask what projects you would be working on in the first six months. Relate your experience to those projects, detailing exactly how you would go about working on them.

- ✔ Give specific examples of your success in dealing with similar projects in the past, focusing on results.

- ✔ Show how crossover skills (also known as *transferable skills*) drawn from even seemingly unrelated experience — such as waiting tables or planning events — apply to this project. You learned the value of being reliable, coordinating efforts, staying organized, and so forth.

Clunkers and Bloopers

> ✔ Say you have no experience. Next question!
>
> ✔ Show that your experience overreaches this particular job — unless you know your overqualification is a plus or when your real agenda is to angle for a higher-level position.

In what ways has your job status changed since you got into this field?

ShowStoppers

> ✔ Mention that you've worked in X number of positions — from small to larger employers — with increasing responsibility; this position is a logical next level in your upward track record.
>
> ✔ Sketch advances in your line of work over the years. Describe how you've continued your education and training to be sure you're moving forward with the technology and the times.
>
> ✔ Draw out hiring objections: Ask whether you failed to cover any key responsibilities. If there's a gap, show how you've handled missing responsibilities, perhaps in earlier positions.

Clunkers and Bloopers

> ✔ Omit mentioning key functions in your move upward. You'll look like you may need to catch up.
>
> ✔ Confirm that you've held the same job for ten years, with little change.

How long would it take you to make a contribution to our company?

ShowStoppers

> ✔ Explain how selecting you will shorten training time because your experience qualifies you as a turnkey candidate. You don't need to be brought up to speed — you've been there and done that job before. Name past challenges, actions, and results.

✔ Estimate how long it would realistically take you to begin producing first-class work on a particular project. Then detail how you would go about working on the project. Forecast how much time you expect each step would take. Be realistic but optimistic in your time estimates.

Clunkers and Bloopers

✔ Say you'll hit the ground running and smile.

✔ State that you can't become productive for at least four months (unless you're headed for an incredibly complex job in which a settling-in period lasting beyond three months is normal).

What are your qualifications?

ShowStoppers

✔ Item by item, connect your close fit between the job's requirements and your qualifications.

✔ Ask what specific projects or problems you may be expected to deal with and which have the highest priority.

✔ Identify the projects you've accomplished in the past that qualify you to work successfully on the projects the interviewer mentions.

Clunkers and Bloopers

✔ Assume you know what the interviewer wants to hear about, plunge in, and fail to check the interviewer's interest after a minute or so.

How did you resolve a tense situation with a co-worker? Have you ever had to fire someone?

ShowStoppers

✔ First, discuss your analytical process for solving routine workplace problems (as advocated in conflict-resolution guidebooks). Storytell a specific example of a problem you solved.

✔ In a termination example, state the steps you took to help the fired person improve and save his job before making a termination decision.

> ✔ Emphasize that you follow company policy and that you're fair and tactful in dealing with employee problems.

Clunkers and Bloopers

> ✔ Complain that colleagues unfairly ganged up on you.
>
> ✔ Discuss an example of when you fired someone because you just didn't like the person.
>
> ✔ Focus on how horrible the problem or employee was, naming names.

Give a specific example of teamwork when you had to put your needs aside to help a co-worker.

ShowStoppers

> ✔ Mention the importance of co-workers being able to rely on each other. Give a specific example, showing how you helped and that the reliance wasn't one-sided.
>
> ✔ Explain in the example that, although you went the extra mile for the team, your efforts didn't cause you to skimp on your own duties. Perhaps you went the extra mile on your own time.

Clunkers and Bloopers

> ✔ Comment that you're a team player and leave it at that.
>
> ✔ Say you can't recall any examples.

What did you like best at your last job?

ShowStoppers

> ✔ Help the interviewer to see a match from past to future by mentioning specific work experiences you were good at and enjoyed that are likely to be present in the prospective position.
>
> ✔ Speak about opportunities to plan your own day or to think out of the box. If you've made a connection, the interviewer may encouragingly say you'll find similar opportunities in this position, and you will enthusiastically agree.

✔ Confirm that you enjoyed being visible in a high-stakes effort, knowing that your contributions directly contributed to the company's bottom line.

Clunkers and Bloopers

✔ Blast your ex-job as a loser and say that's why you're here.

✔ Explain that nothing stands out as having been especially rewarding.

Describe a time that you had to work without direct supervision. Have you ever had to make department decisions when your supervisor was not available?

ShowStoppers

✔ Discuss your level-headed decision-making process. You don't rattle easily.

✔ Show that you're self-directed and self-motivated, but are happily willing to follow others' directions or to ask for assistance when needed.

✔ Storytell: Discuss a specific example of a time you had to make a decision without supervision. Choose an instance when you anticipated company needs and finished a project ahead of time or made a beneficial decision.

Clunkers and Bloopers

✔ Whine about being forced into a decision that turned sour.

✔ Admit that you've never worked without someone looking over your shoulder or telling you what to do.

Have you ever misjudged something? How could you have prevented the mistake?

ShowStoppers

✔ Briefly discuss a specific — but minor — example of misjudgment. Say what the mistake taught you and how it led you to improve your system for making decisions or solving problems.

✔ After talking about your example and what you learned from it, ask a question to refocus the discussion on your accomplishments — "Would you like to hear about a notable win as well as that loss?"

Clunkers and Bloopers

✔ Discuss a mistake that cost your employer plenty of time and money.

✔ Pass the blame to someone else.

✔ Say you've never misjudged anything.

Has a supervisor ever challenged one of your decisions? How did you respond?

ShowStoppers

✔ Identify an example of being challenged when you listened politely but supported your decision with research or analytical data, and you won over your critical supervisor.

✔ Add that even though you justified your decision, you were open to suggestions and comments. You're confident in your abilities but not closed minded or foolishly stubborn.

Clunkers and Bloopers

✔ Castigate your supervisor for trying to micromanage.

✔ Insist that you were right even though management reversed your decision.

In your current position, what are your three most important accomplishments?

ShowStoppers

✔ Mention six of your best work accomplishment stories. Ask which ones the interviewer would like to hear more about.

✔ After describing the top three, comment that you can expand the list and reach across the desk to hand over an accomplishment sheet with your name, contact information, and as many as ten accomplishments. (Leave your accomplishment sheet behind as a reminder of your talents.)

Clunkers and Bloopers

> ✔ Laughingly remark that you have so many accomplishments that it's hard to choose just three.

> ✔ Admit that you're not sure what counts as an accomplishment.

Your experience doesn't exactly match our needs right now, does it?

ShowStoppers

> ✔ Don't agree. Instead, state that you see your fit with the job through a rosier lens. Your skills are cross-functional. Focus on how you can easily transfer your experience in related areas to learning this new job.

> ✔ Stress that you're dedicated to learning the new job quickly. Give two true examples of how you learned a job skill much faster than usual.

> ✔ Say you don't have any bad habits to unlearn and discuss your good work habits that will help you get the job done efficiently and well.

Clunkers and Bloopers

> ✔ Agree, smile, and say nothing to compensate for the mismatch — unless, of course, you don't want the job.

> ✔ Let the door hit you on the way out.

Dealing with the Premature Salary Question

Just when the interview is starting to fly, *bam!* — the interviewer lets go with a dangerous question that can severely clip your wings: *How much money are you looking for?* Should you name your price right then and there? Not if you can help it. If you have to talk salary too early in the interviewing process, a decision maker may not yet be sufficiently smitten with you to make the company's best offer.

Delay discussing salary until you're offered (or nearly offered) a specific position. Until you have the offer, the employer holds all the weight. After you have the offer, the scales shift. You have something the employer wants, and you become equals negotiating a business proposition. From outsider, you have become poised to become the newest insider — a good place to be.

Learning to deflect salary questions until the timing shifts to your advantage can greatly influence the amount of money that you take from the bargaining table.

Stalling money talk the smart way

Although the advice to sit tight until the timing is right is still on the mark, doing so is easier said than done these days, says salary negotiation expert extraordinaire Jack Chapman (www.salarynegotiations.com). He explains:

> *In the 1980s, it was easy to postpone the salary talk. That has changed over the years. Employers are more demanding or inquisitive or something. Yet the principle is the same — postpone when and if you can.*

But when you're pressured to talk money sooner rather than later, Chapman warns that digging in your heels and flat-out refusing to comply is a mistake. By being hard-nosed, you set up a power struggle that you can't win. You'll be seen as obstinate and hard to work with. Nor should you move to the other extreme, in which you meekly cave in, tell all, and let it go at that. A roll-over-and-scratch-my-belly response may make you seem too weak.

Moreover, when you're too low or too high for the company's budget, you hand the employer's interviewing screener information to judge you by your price, not by your whole package of qualifications. Even in the final interview round, premature dollars talk may lead a decision maker to see you as too expensive without your being given an opportunity to justify your worth and negotiate.

Fortunately, there's a better way to connect when you're giving away your bargaining leverage too soon: Get a quid pro quo. I think of this kind of fair exchange as Chapman's rule:

> *When you comply with an early request for your salary numbers, get markers in return. Something for something.*

What markers do you want as IOUs for your upfront compliance? You want agreement that your early money talk won't screen you out of further interview opportunities. And you want agreement that your salary discussion will focus on the market value of the position and not on your salary history.

To side-step the negative consequences of early revelation as much as possible, you want fair consideration. Here are Chapman's illustrations of what you can say to get fair consideration in three interviewing situations:

- ✔ **Phone screening:** *Before I give you all that information, can I ask a question? (Yes.) I don't know who you'll hire, but from what I've seen so far, you should definitely at least interview me. If I'm forthright about all my compensation factors, can I be assured of an interview?*

- ✔ **Interview screening:** *Before I give you all that information, can I ask a question? (Yes.) I don't know who you'll hire, but from what I've seen so far, I would definitely like to participate in the second round of interviews. If I'm forthright about all my compensation factors, can I be assured of that?*

- ✔ **Selection interviewing:** *Before I give you all that information, can I ask a question? (Yes.) I'm a little concerned that we could lose a perfectly good match over salary expectations. And I'm confident that you'll pay a competitive salary — which is all I need. Can you first give me your rough range, your ballpark compensation, and I'll be candid and tell you how that compares?*

If you're too high or too low, Chapman's approach gives you the opportunity to address the discrepancy in the interview process instead of having the employer decide behind closed doors with no input from you.

Alternatively, you can try to gracefully hold off a salary discussion. The following replies give you ideas for how to respond to premature questions about your salary expectations:

✔ *I'm sure that money won't be a problem after I'm able to show you how my qualifications can work to your advantage because they closely match your requirements.*

✔ *My salary requirements are open to discussion. Your company has a reputation of being fair with employees, and I trust you would do the same in my case. I don't think salary will be a problem if I'm the right person for the job.*

✔ *I'm aware of the general range for my kind of work, but I'd feel better talking about pay once we've established what specific performance goals the job calls for.*

✔ *I'd be kidding if I said money isn't important to me — sure, it is! But the job itself and the work environment are also very important to me. I wonder if we can hold the pay issue for a bit?*

✔ *I'm a great believer in matching pay with performance, so I can't speak with any certainty about the kind of money I'm looking for until I know more about what you need.*

✔ *Money is not my only priority; I'd really like to discuss my contributions to the company first — if that's okay with you.*

✔ *I can't answer that question until I know more about this job.*

✔ *The amount of my starting compensation is not as much of an issue to me as how satisfying my filling the position will be for both of us. Can we talk more about what the position entails?*

✔ *Before we get into the compensation issue, can you tell me more about the kind of skills and the type of individual you're looking for to help you reach your goals? What do you expect the person you hire to accomplish within the first three months?*

✔ *All I need is fair market value for the job's demands, which I'm sure you'll pay, so is it okay if we talk about the details of the job first?*

✔ *As far as I can tell, the position seems like a perfect fit for me — tit for tat on your requirements and my qualifications. So as long as you pay in the industry ballpark, I'm sure that we won't have a problem coming up with a figure we're both happy with.*

✔ *Before we can come to an agreement, I need to know more about your strategy for compensation, as well as confirm my understanding of the results you're looking for. Can we hold that question for a bit?*

✔ *Since pay includes so many possibilities for compensation, I'd like to first know more about your compensation plan overall and how it relates to the position.*

✔ *I'm sure that you have a fair salary structure, and if I'm the best candidate for the position, we can work something out that we'll all like.*

✔ *I'm not used to talking money before a job offer; are you making me an offer?*

✔ *My requirement is market within the area — shouldn't be a problem. Can we put that off to the side until we decide if there's any need to go further down the money road?*

✔ *I will consider any reasonable offer. Should we talk about it after we've wrapped up the details of the job, and I've been able to show you what I bring to your company?*

✔ *I'm paid roughly the market value of a (occupational title) with (number of years') experience and the ability to (manage, or do something special). If you're competitive with the market, there won't be a problem with salary.*

Knowing market pay rates just in case

Knowing your *market value* — the going rate for people in your industry with skills and a job description similar to yours — is the centerpiece for negotiating the compensation you deserve.

Discovering the market rate for the kind of work you do has never been easier than it is today. Among popular websites offering free salary survey information to job seekers are Salary.com (`www.salary.com`) and Payscale (`www.pay scale.com`).

Another very useful free resource is the job search engine Indeed.com (`www.indeed.com`), which reports actual salary ranges currently posted on job boards.

Generalized averages produced by online salary calculators aren't always spot-on for specific companies and jobs.

Be certain to benchmark the job you're applying for by *job content* — not just by job title. The same job title can mean different things to different people in different companies.

Handling Questions about a Special Situation

The actual reasons candidates are rejected (other than the commonly given reason of losing out to a better prepared candidate) often relate to special situations. These range from a mild to a serious stumbling block in the interviewer's perception. Sometimes the special issues are discussed, but often they remain unspoken.

Perhaps you've been in the same job too long, making you appear to be unmotivated. Maybe you have employment gaps or the opposite — too many previous jobs hanging around your neck. Sometimes you're pretty sure that you're running into rejection because you were fired for cause or demoted.

 Think carefully before discussing special issues. Even a question that seems innocent may cause you to reveal things you didn't mean to tell. For nonsensitive questions, asking for more time to think about your answer is okay. But for special-issue answers, you seem more straightforward and sure of yourself when you anticipate the question and are ready with a good answer.

The following sections provide comments and response strategies to help shape your special issue to your advantage.

When you've long been in the same job

What some may consider stability, others may see as fossilization. Your chief strategy when you've had the same job for years and years is to look industrious, ready to take on any challenge that comes your way, and adaptable to new ideas.

Because you've been with your last employer for so long, do you think you may have a hard time adjusting to a new company's way of working?

ShowStoppers

> ✔ Not at all. Give examples of how you've already learned to be adaptable — how your previous job was dynamic, provided a constantly changing environment, and shared common links with the new company. Note parallels of budget, business philosophy, and work ethics. You plan to take up mountain climbing and sky diving when you're 80 — figuratively speaking.

> ✔ Emphasize your commitment to your previous company as one of many assets you bring with you to the new position — and then name more of your assets.

Clunkers and Bloopers

> ✔ Discuss your relief at escaping that old awful job — at last!

> ✔ Simply say you're ready to try something new.

You've been in your previous position an unusually long period of time — why haven't you been promoted?

ShowStoppers

> ✔ Present the old job in modules (by clusters of skills you developed rather than by your periods of employment). Concentrate on all increases in responsibility (to show upward mobility within the position) and on relevant accomplishments. Note raises.

> ✔ Say that you're interested in this new job precisely because of the inertia of your previous position. Mention any lifestyle changes (grown kids, second family income) freeing you to make a vigorous move at this time.

> ✔ Agree that your career hasn't progressed much, but note that many talented people are forced to root or to accept lateral moves because few upwardly mobile job slots are available. Say your career plateau gave you time to reflect and solidify your skills set, lighting a fire under your motivation.

> ✔ Explain that you reached the highest position the company offered individuals in your specialty.

Clunkers and Bloopers

> ✔ Complain about office politics keeping you down.
>
> ✔ Say you were happy where you were and ask, "Why fix what isn't broken?"

When you're shoved out the door

The number-one rule in explaining why you were fired is to keep it brief, keep it honest, and keep it moving. Say what you need to say and redirect the conversation to your qualifications. As for what you should say, you have two core options.

Were you fired from your last job?

ShowStoppers

> ✔ **If it wasn't your fault:**
>
> Explain the firing as a result of downsizing, mergers, company closure, or some other act beyond your control. Sometimes firing happens several times in a row to good people who figuratively happen to be standing on the wrong street corner when the wrong bus comes along and runs them over. Being let go wasn't your fault, so you have no reason to feel guilty. Get on with the interview with a sincere smile on your face.
>
> ✔ **If it was your fault:**
>
> Say you learned an enormous lesson during the experience. You messed up, but you know better now, and you won't make the same mistakes again. Explain briefly how you benefited from this learning experience. Then quickly turn the interview back to the better you and go on to explain how you're the hands-down best candidate for the job.

Clunkers and Bloopers

> ✔ Give interviewers the impression that you're hiding something, that you're not being absolutely honest and open with them.
>
> ✔ Bad-mouth your former boss. Say your former co-workers were a freak show.

> ✔ Tell the interviewer that you've had personality conflicts on more than one job. That admission sets off screaming smoke detectors warning that you're a fiery troublemaker.

Have you ever been asked to resign? Why?

ShowStoppers

> ✔ Being allowed to resign (a soft firing) suggests that you may be able to work out a mutually agreeable rationale with your former employer. Do so and stick to the story the two of you come up with.
>
> ✔ When you have no good storyline, admit your mistake and say it was a painful lesson that caused a change in your work habits.

Clunkers and Bloopers

> ✔ Lie or give excuses to justify why you shouldn't have been treated so unfairly.
>
> ✔ Rip on your ex-bosses or co-workers for forcing you out.
>
> ✔ Give multiple examples of your interpersonal conflicts.

When sexual orientation is up for discussion

A growing number of U.S. companies are expanding benefits and protections for their gay, lesbian, bisexual, and transgendered (GLBT) employees. Even the U.S. military is keeping pace with this trend by repealing the "don't ask, don't tell" ban on gay men and women serving openly in the military.

The movement to include GLBT workers in anti-discrimination policies includes two key points:

> ✔ Offering same-sex couples the same benefits as straight couples
>
> ✔ Seeking out potential GLBT workers in company recruiting

Don't be lulled into complacent mistakes because of the rapid acceleration in the GLBT equality movement. (Shockingly, being gay is not a legally recognized protected class.)

Here are suggestions to smooth away wrinkles from your interviewing experience if you're a member of the GLBT community:

✔ If you choose to disclose, wait until either the interviewer shows enormous interest in your qualifications and you know an offer is imminent or the offer is actually made. (Some savvy advisers recommend that you wait until you have a written offer letter in hand.)

✔ Thoroughly research the company's culture and civil rights policies before the interview. Look for companies that proclaim a nondiscriminatory policy on sexual orientation. Look for a company that offers life partners a domestic partner benefits plan.

✔ How can you tell whether equality-happy talk is real or window dressing? Ask members of GLBT support networks what they know about a company where you plan to interview. Browse for GLBT job boards and websites.

Although you won't be asked directly about your sexual orientation, an interviewer may — inadvertently or purposely — nibble around the edges with inappropriate personal questions.

Is there a special woman in your life? How's your marriage?

ShowStoppers

✔ **A nondisclosure answer:** You consider a number of women special in your life (meaning your mother, your sister, and your aunt), or just say you're not married yet.

✔ **A confirming but neutral answer:** Say you're gay, open with your family and friends, and in a stable relationship. You may also want to casually mention that your sexual orientation has no bearing on the quality of your work. Add that it's not a problem for you and that you hope it isn't a problem for the company. (Being open suggests that you're not anxious and preoccupied about being exposed, that you have the support of your family, and that you're emotionally stable and strong.)

Clunkers and Bloopers

🖊 Bluntly refuse to discuss your personal life.

🖊 Ask whether the interviewer is married.

I see that when you were a college student, you were president for two years of the campus Gay-Straight Alliance Group — can you tell me about that?

ShowStoppers

🖊 Note that Gay-Straight alliances are found on campuses nationwide, functioning as anti-discrimination organizations. On your campus, the Gay-Straight Alliance Group has 75 (or correct number) members. As president, you were the group's representative in student government and participated in official greeting events with visiting dignitaries. All your duties weren't so visible — you also led planning for fundraising activities, balanced the checkbook, and helped clean up after events.

🖊 Explain that, after leading the Gay-Straight Alliance Group as president for two years, you received a Campus Leader Award from the university's chancellor; ask whether the interviewer would like to see it (from your portfolio).

Clunkers and Bloopers

🖊 Answer only that it was a political action group for GLBT students.

🖊 Say that you led angry protests at school events.

When you've worked everywhere

In an era of contract workers, just-in-time temporary hirings, and companies tossing employees overboard to boost already healthy profits for stockholders, I'm always surprised to hear employers object to "job hopping." I shouldn't be.

Employers favor candidates with a track record of staying a "reasonable" amount of time at previous jobs. They assume that the past predicts the future and that the candidate will stay as long as he's wanted at the company. The kicker is the meaning of "reasonable amount of time." The current group-think narrative places a minimum stay in a job at two to three years.

This arbitrary time frame doesn't mean you shouldn't cut your losses and leave if you're in a bad job — circumstances vary widely. It does, however, mean you should give plenty of thought to how you handle a job-hopper question and deal with it in a logical, convincing, and upbeat manner.

You've changed jobs more frequently than is usual — why is that?

ShowStoppers

- ✔ List accomplishments in each job that relate to the position you seek. Note that you built new skills in each job. Say that you're a person who contributes value wherever you go.

- ✔ Give acceptable, verifiable reasons why you changed jobs so frequently — project-oriented work, downsizing, dead-end positions, company sold out, or department shut down.

- ✔ Say that you've become more selective lately, and you hadn't been able to find the right job until this opportunity came along; explain your employment travels as a quest for a fulfilling job.

- ✔ If this move is a career change for you, show how your experience and skills support this change and how the position fits your revised career goals.

- ✔ If your positions were for temporary agencies, cluster the jobs by responsibility and recast them as evidence of your use of cross-functional skills in many situations. You're a Renaissance man or woman.

- ✔ Ask whether this is regular-status employment. If so, admit you've lacked some commitment in the past, but now you're ready to settle down with a good company, such as this one. If not, say a temporary job is just what you have in mind to keep your skills refreshed with experiences gained at various companies.

Clunkers and Bloopers

> ✔ Complain about what was wrong with each of your ex-employers that made you quit. Say you didn't want to waste your time working for dysfunctional people and organizations.
>
> ✔ Show a lack of focus — you just couldn't get into your jobs.
>
> ✔ Say you're looking for something that pays more.

When gaps drill holes in your history

Employers may rush to judgment when they find gaps in your job history. If your job history has as many gaps as a hockey player's smile, try to find growth experiences (self-directed study or education by travel).

If you must blame your jobless patches on sick leave, emphasize that you have fully recovered and are in excellent health. If personal problems take the hit (ill parent or sick child), follow up with facts that indicate the personal problems are history.

When your record is spotty beyond belief, try to get on with a temporary job and then prove by your work record that you've turned over a new leaf.

Sometimes the gaps in your record are of recent vintage — you've been looking for employment without success for a very long time. In current periods of unemployment, your posture is commitment — you throw yourself heart and soul into your work and you want to be very sure to find a good fit. Explain your waiting period as a quest for a fulfilling job.

How long have you been job hunting? Wow! That's a long time — what's the problem? Why haven't you had any job offers yet?

ShowStoppers

> ✔ Say you've become more selective lately, and you hadn't been able to find the right job until this opportunity came along.

✔ If you were given a sizable severance package, explain how it financially allowed you to take your time searching for the perfect next move.

✔ Admit your career hasn't progressed as much as you'd like, but the good news is that you've had time to think through your life direction, you've reassessed your career, and you feel focused now. You're fueled up and ready to go!

✔ Explain that although you're good at building consensus (through compromise) with others, you haven't been willing to settle for a job that doesn't maximize your skills and qualifications. Say that low-end jobs are all that have turned up in this market until now. Clarify that you've taken your time to find the perfect job fit because the position is very important to you.

Clunkers and Bloopers

✔ Say you don't know what the problem is.

✔ Complain that greedy employers are beating up on the working class.

✔ Gripe about how many opportunities you've missed out on because recruiters don't recognize your true worth.

✔ Look depressed and admit that you're becoming discouraged.

When you're demoted a notch

Demotion carries more negative baggage than does firing. Demotion suggests personal failure; firing doesn't, unless you're fired for cause.

Do I read this resume right — were you demoted?

ShowStoppers

✔ Your best move is to deal with demotions before you reach the interview. Ask your demoting boss for a positive reference and come to an agreement about what happened that's favorable to you — assuming your boss knows you're looking around and doesn't mind helping you leave.

- ✔ Explain honestly and as positively as possible the reasons for your send-down.

- ✔ Admit that you weren't ready for the responsibility at that time, but now you are. My, how you've grown! Describe the actions you've taken to grow professionally — school courses in deficient areas, management seminars, management books, and introspection.

- ✔ Affirm that you're looking for a good place to put your new and improved management skills to use, and you hope that place is where you're interviewing. Quickly remind interviewers that you're qualified for the job you're interviewing for, and back that up with examples of your skills and quantified achievements.

Clunkers and Bloopers

- ✔ Lie or try to shift the blame to anybody but you.

- ✔ Accuse management of unreasonable expectations.

Answering a Questionable Question

Employers shouldn't quiz you about any of the following topics:

- ✔ Age

- ✔ Birthplace

- ✔ Color

- ✔ Disability

- ✔ Marital/family status

- ✔ National origin

- ✔ Race

- ✔ Religion

- ✔ Sex (gender)

Federal, state, and city laws prohibit employers from asking certain questions unrelated to the job they're hiring to fill.

Questions should be job related, not used to pry loose personal information. Some inquiries about the off-limits topics are flat-out illegal. Others are merely borderline and inappropriate.

Illegal questions are always inappropriate, but inappropriate questions aren't always illegal. I help you distinguish between illegal and inappropriate questions (and run through several questions interviewers should never ask) in the next sections.

Defining illegal questions

An *illegal* question is one that the interviewer has no legal right to ask. The federal government and most states and large cities have laws restraining employers from going hog-wild with intrusive questions. These laws cover civil rights — age, sex, religion, race, ethnicity, sexual orientation, and so forth. Asking illegal questions can get the interviewer called on the legal carpet.

Club Fed's forbidden questions

Discrimination law is ever changing and complex. Contrary to popular understanding, there's no such thing as a list of questions prohibited by federal law, except for these two:

✓ **Have you ever been arrested?** An employer can't ask about your arrest record because an arrest isn't an admission of guilt. But asking about an individual's convictions — *Have you ever been convicted of a crime?* — is okay.

✓ **How's your health?** The Americans with Disabilities Act forbids pre-employment questions asking about a candidate's health. But asking about an

individual's ability to perform job-related tasks — *Can you stand for long periods of time?* — is okay.

Other than these two questions, interviewers can ask any questions they wish as far as the federal government is concerned. (Of course, they ultimately may pay a stiff penalty for bias if you file a claim that sticks.)

Federal law merely notes subjects — based on disability and civil rights, such as visible and invisible impairments, race, sex, age, and so on — that can be the basis for bias complaints and prohibits discriminatory treatment on these grounds.

To find out what's what in your locale, snag the facts.

- ✔ You can inquire at your state or city attorney general's office. Check out a big library for a list of questions that shouldn't be asked, especially according to state or local laws.
- ✔ At the federal level, scout the website of the U.S. Equal Employment Opportunity Commission (www.eeoc.gov; search for "Federal Laws Prohibiting Job Discrimination: Questions and Answers").
- ✔ Browse online for "list of illegal job interview questions."

Defining inappropriate questions

An *inappropriate* question is one the interviewer can legally ask but probably shouldn't. Depending on whether the information is used to discriminate, inappropriate questions set up employers for lawsuits. It's a threat their corporate lawyers constantly warn against. Inappropriate questions range from civil rights and privacy issues to hard-to-classify bizarre inquiries, such as

Is your girlfriend white?

How would you go about making a pizza?

If you were at a department meeting and a co-worker put his hand on your thigh, what would you do?

Interviewers in companies that have human resources departments should know better than to ask inappropriate questions. But some go on fishing expeditions, hoping that weird, unexpected questions will rattle candidates and cause them to "show their true colors." Other interviewers are natural-born buttinskies who ask risky questions because they want the information and are willing to gamble that they won't be challenged.

Rehearsing dicey questions

Table 4-1 is a playbill of inappropriate or illegal questions you hope you never hear. Decide in advance how you'll respond to nonstarters like these — just in case. When the quizzing is expressed in an appropriate version, as noted in the right-hand column, give a straightforward answer.

Table 4-1	Questions Interviewers Shouldn't Ask	
Topic	**_Inappropriate or Illegal Questions_**	**_Appropriate Versions_**
Age	What is your date of birth? How old are you?	If hired, can you furnish proof that you are over age 18?
Arrest and conviction	Have you ever been arrested?	Have you ever been convicted of a crime? If so, when, where, and what was the disposition of the case?
Citizenship/ national origin	What is your national origin? Where are your parents from?	Are you legally eligible for employment in the United States?
Credit record	Have your wages ever been garnished? Have you ever declared bankruptcy?	Credit questions can be used if they comply with the Fair Credit Reporting Act of 1970 and the Consumer Credit Reporting Reform Act of 1996.
Disabilities	Do you have any disabilities?	Can you perform the duties of the job you are applying for?
Education	When did you graduate from high school or college?	Do you have a high school diploma or equivalent? Do you have a university or college degree?
Family	How many children do you have? Who's going to baby-sit? Do you have preschool-age children at home? What is your marital status?	What hours and days can you work? Do you have responsibilities other than work that will interfere with specific job requirements, such as traveling?
Home	Do you own your home?	None.
Language	What is your native language? How did you learn to read, write, or speak a foreign language?	Which languages do you speak and write fluently? (If the job requires additional languages)

(continued)

Table 4-1 *(continued)*

Topic	Inappropriate or Illegal Questions	Appropriate Versions
Military record	What type of discharge did you receive?	What type of education, training, and work experience did you receive while in the military?
Organizations	Which clubs, societies, and lodges do you belong to? Are you a union member?	Are you a member of an organization that you consider relevant to your ability to perform the job?
Personal	What color are your eyes and hair? What is your weight?	Permissible only if there is a bona fide occupational qualification.
Pregnancy	Your application says that your status is married. Do your plans include starting a family soon?	None.
Religion	What is your religious denomination or religious affiliation? What church do you attend? What is your parish, and who is your pastor? Which religious holidays do you observe?	Are there specific times you cannot work?
Worker's compensation	Have you ever filed for worker's compensation? Have you had any prior work injuries?	None.

Chapter 5

Asking the Right Questions at the Right Times

In This Chapter

▶ Knowing when to ask work-related questions

▶ Being careful with questions about the employer's performance

*S*o you just finished answering a seemingly endless line of questions about your work history and your education, and you're pretty confident that you held your own. Now the interviewer turns to you and asks, "Do you have any questions?" That's your cue to ask how much money you're gonna make at this outfit anyway, right? Wrong!

The types of questions you ask and when you ask them are the least understood parts of the job interview, but there are really only two basic categories:

  ✔ **Questions that sell you:** These questions help you get an offer; they're a way to sell without selling.

  ✔ **Questions that address your personal agenda:** These questions about pay, benefits, and other self-interest items need to be asked only after you receive an offer — or at least a heavy hint of an offer.

In this chapter, I focus on the types of questions you should ask prior to receiving a job offer.

Asking Selling Questions before the Offer

For all jobs, asking about anything other than work issues before a hiring offer comes your way is a serious strategic error. The interviewer, particularly a hiring manager who resents the time "diverted" from typical duties to an interview, is totally uninterested in your needs at this point. What's important to the interviewer is solving the hiring problem. *First we decide, then we deal* — that's the thinking.

To talk about your needs before an offer turns the interviewer's mind to negative thoughts: All you want is money, insurance, and a nice vacation on the company. You're not interested in doing the job.

 Keep your focus on the employer's needs and how you can meet them. Sell yourself by asking questions that are centered on the work, tasks, and functions.

 Ask about the position's duties and challenges. Ask what outcomes you're expected to produce. Ask how the position fits into the department, and the department into the company. Ask about typical assignments. Here are examples of work-related questions:

- ✔ What would be my first project if I were hired for this position?

- ✔ What would my key responsibilities be?

- ✔ Who (and how many) would I supervise? To whom would I report?

- ✔ Would I be working as a member of a team?

- ✔ What percentage of time would I spend communicating with customers, co-workers, and managers?

- ✔ Would on-the-job training be required for a new product?

- ✔ Can you describe a typical day?

- ✔ Was the last person in this job promoted? What's the potential for promotion?

- How would you describe the atmosphere here? Formal and traditional? Energetically informal?

- Where is the company headed? Merger? Growth?

- What type of training would I receive?

- What resources would I have to do the job?

- How much would I travel, if any?

- (If a contract job) Do you anticipate extensive overtime to finish the project on schedule?

- Where does this position fit into the company's organizational structure?

- What results would you expect from my efforts and on what timetable? What improvements need to be made on how the job has been done until now?

How much time should you invest in asking selling questions? Five to ten minutes. Gregory J. Walling, a top executive recruiter based in Alexandria, Virginia, says he's never heard an employer complain about a candidate being too interested in work.

 Don't ask questions about information you can glean from research. Portraying yourself as an A-list candidate and then asking "lazy questions" doesn't leave a favorable impression.

Drawing Out Hidden Objections

The questions you ask have one more mission: They're a good way to smoke out hidden concerns or objections that may keep you from finishing first in the competition.

Reasons that employers hang back with unspoken anxieties often relate to legal vulnerability, or the interviewer may simply be uncomfortable asking about them. Whatever the reason, silent concerns are hurdles standing in the way of you getting the job. Before the interview is over, find a way to address any thorny issues and overcome them.

Good salespeople call techniques that do this "drawing out objections." After you know the issues that — under the surface — are chilling your chances, try calling them out.

One of the best questions I've ever heard to jar loose unspoken doubts was passed on by legendry recruiting authority and author John Lucht (www.ritesite.com). When the interview is about four-fifths complete, Lucht suggests you ask this question: *What do you think would be the biggest challenge for someone with my background coming into this position?*

Here's your golden opportunity to bury any concerns on the spot or in your thank-you letter. (If you can't collect your thoughts quickly enough, at least you'll have a clue for your next interview after you know what may be holding back employers from choosing you.)

Treading Lightly around Employer-Performance Questions

Although you need as much information as possible to make good job choices, asking a potential boss questions like "How would you describe your management style?" or "Do your employees admire you as a boss?" in the wrong tone of voice may make you seem way too audacious. Moreover, direct questions about personal characteristics and values tend to elicit pure topspin.

Instead, ask questions designed to draw out companywide anecdotal answers:

- ✔ How did the company handle a recent downsizing?
- ✔ How did managers react to someone who took a stand on principle?
- ✔ Who are the company's heroes?

This approach encourages conversation that can be very informative.

Questions are tools. Use them wisely.

Chapter 6

Closing on a High Note

· ·

In This Chapter

▶ Ensuring you leave the interview in a positive light

▶ Saying thanks and pursuing the job without being a pest

▶ Improving future interviews with a post-interview checklist

· ·

*H*ow can you be sure an interview is almost over? Watch for these nonverbal clues: The interviewer may begin shuffling papers, glancing at a wall clock or watch, stretching silences, and standing up. Then you hear words that confirm your hunch:

✔ *Thanks for coming in. We'll be interviewing more candidates through the next week or so. After that, I'll probably get back to you about a second interview.*

✔ *Thanks for talking with me. I think your qualifications make you a definite candidate for this position. When I'm done with all the initial interviews, I'll get back to you.*

✔ *All your input has been really helpful. Now that I know everything I need to know about you, do you have any questions about the company or the position?*

In this chapter, I reveal your best exit lines and remind you to exhibit friendly confidence, no matter how the interviewer behaves.

Making a Strategic Exit

Do yourself a favor by never leaving a job interview empty-handed. Instead of quietly fading into history, memorize these four important points:

✔ Immerse your departure in *interactive selling*. Sales professionals use this term to mean a great deal of back and forth, give and take, and questions and answers. You're alive!

✔ Reprise your qualifications and the benefits you bring to the job. You're a great match and a wonderful fit, and you'll be quickly productive.

✔ Find out what happens next in the hiring process. Mysteries are for crime show viewers.

✔ Prop open the door for your follow-up. Without paving the way, you may seem desperate when you call back to see what's up.

Your parting sales pitch

Haven't you sold yourself enough? Yes and no. People — including interviewers — often forget what they hear. Start your close with another chorus of your five best skills. (See Chapter 4 for answers to the question, "Why should I hire you?") Then ask

> *Do you see any gaps between my qualifications and the requirements for the job?*
>
> *Based on what we've discussed today, do you have any concerns about my ability to do well in this job? Any reservations about hiring me?*

You're looking for gaps and hidden objections so you can make them seem insignificant. But if the gaps aren't wide and the objections aren't lethal to your candidacy, attempt to overcome stated shortcomings. You can make this attempt based on what you found out in your earlier research. Here's an effective formula you can use to *engage the interviewer:*

1. **Sell your qualifications (skills and other requirements for the job).**

2. **Ask for objections.**

3. **Listen carefully.**

4. **Overcome objections.**

5. **Restate your qualifications using different words.**

So how hard should you sell? It all depends.

- ✔ When you're in a sales field, lack experience in a job's requirements, or aren't obviously superior to your competition, don't hold back on selling your advantages or showing your enthusiasm.

- ✔ When you have relevant experience and offer in-demand skills or are being considered for a senior-level job, allow yourself to be wooed a bit. You don't want to be seen as jumping at every opportunity.

- ✔ When the gap between your qualifications and the job's requirements is the size of the Grand Canyon, accept the fact that the job will go to someone else.

- ✔ When you just don't have the chops for the position, salvage your time and effort by acknowledging that although you may not be ideal for this particular position, interviewing for it has caused you to admire the company and its people. You'd appreciate being contacted if a better match comes along.

After you restate your qualifications, you may find the time is ripe to reaffirm your interest in the job and subtly lead toward an offer. Here's one example to illustrate how such a scenario might play out:

> *I hope I've answered your concerns on the X issue. Do you have further questions or issues about my background, qualifications, or anything else at this point? This job and I sound like a terrific match.*

Depending upon the interviewer's response, make your move.

> *I hope you agree that this position has my name on it. As I understand, your position requires X, and I can deliver X; your position requires Y, and I can deliver Y; your position requires Z, and I can deliver Z.*

> *So there seems to be a good match here! Don't you think so?*

> *I'm really glad I had the chance to talk with you. I know that with what I learned at Violet Tech when I established its Internet website, I can set up an excellent website for you, too.*

Leaving the door open

How can you prop the door open for a follow-up? You seek the interviewer's permission to call back; with permission, you won't seem intrusive. Use these statements as models to gain the permission:

> *What's the next step in the hiring process, and when do you expect to make a decision?* (You're trying to get a sense of the timetable.)

> *I'm quite enthusiastic about this position. When and how do we take the next step?*

> *May I call if I have further questions? Or would you prefer that I e-mail or text you?*

> *I know you're not done reviewing candidates; when can I reach you to check up on the progress of your search?*

> *I understand you'll call me back after you've seen every candidate for this position; would you mind if I call you for an update or if I have more questions?*

> *I appreciate the time you spent with me; I know you're going to be really busy recruiting, so when can I call you?*

> *I look forward to that second interview you mentioned — can I call you later to schedule it after my work hours so I don't have to throw off my current employer's schedule?*

> *You say I'm the leading candidate for this position. Terrific! That's great to hear —when shall we talk again?*

In the final moments, be certain to express thanks to the interviewer for the time spent with you. Say it with a smile, eye-to-nose, and a firm but gentle handshake: *This position looks like a terrific opportunity and a great fit for me — I look forward to hearing from you.* Then leave. Don't linger.

As soon as you're alone at a place where you can make notes, write a summary of the meeting. Concentrate especially on material for your follow-up moves, described in the next section.

Follow Up or Fall Behind

What takes place after the first selection interview — when candidates are ranked — decides who has the inside track on winning the job.

Your follow-up may be the tiebreaker that gives you the win over other promising candidates. And even if the employer already planned to offer you the job, your follow-up creates goodwill that kick-starts your success when you join the company.

Follow up vigorously. It's your caring that counts. Your basic tools are

- ✔ Print letters
- ✔ E-mails
- ✔ Telephone calls

Letters

How much do *post-interview* thank-you letters really impact hiring decisions? It depends on the letter.

When your letter is canned, flat, routine, boring, and of the "Dear Aunt Martha, Thanks for the graduation gift" model, interviewers may yawn and toss it.

But when your letter is a persuasive self-marketing communication masquerading as a thank-you letter, interviewers are likely to pay attention to you as a thoughtful and conscientious top contender.

Get started with the following content capsules for your thanks/marketing letter aimed at converting your candidacy into a job offer:

- ✔ Express appreciation for the interviewer's time and for giving you a fresh update on the organization's immediate direction.

- ✔ Remind the interviewer of what specifically you can do for the company, not what the company can do for you. As you did in closing your interview, draw links between the company's immediate needs and your qualifications: "You want X, I offer X; you want Y, I offer Y; you want Z, I offer Z."

✔ Repeat your experience in handling concerns that were discussed during the interview. Write very brief paragraphs about how you solved problems of interest to the company.

✔ Tie up loose ends by adding information to a question you didn't handle well during the interview.

✔ Overcome objections the interviewer expressed about offering you the job. For example, if the job has an international component and the interviewer was concerned that you've never worked in Europe or Asia, explain that you've worked productively in other cultures, notably the Caribbean and in Mexico.

✔ Reaffirm your interest in the position and respect for the company.

Generally, a follow-up letter is most effective when limited to one page with five to seven short paragraphs. But a killer letter can run two, or even three, pages if it's flush with white space, easy to read, and written for a professional-level position.

E-mail

In this digital age, an e-mail follow-up is fine for most jobs. Consider these observations on communicating after an interview by e-mail:

✔ E-mail is more conversational and easier for a quick reply. On the other hand, it's also easier to say *no* in an e-mail message than on the telephone.

✔ Use e-mail if that's the way you sent your resume and especially if the employer requested electronic communication in a job ad.

✔ Use e-mail when you're dealing with a high-tech firm; the firm's hiring authority probably doesn't remember what paper is and may think voicemail is a bother.

Don't make blanket assumptions about whether spam filters will prevent your message from reaching the interviewer. Instead, ask the interviewer or a receptionist in advance about the best way to send an e-mail message.

When you get a job offer at the interview

With an offer on the table, bring up your self-interest requests for information (think vacation, benefits, lunch hours, and so on). Whip out a note pad and say,

I'm excited and grateful for your interest. I'd like to clear up just a few issues. Can you tell me about — ?

Unless the circumstances are unusual, accepting or rejecting a job offer on the spot is not in your best interest. You're likely to think of something later that you forgot to negotiate, and improving an offer after you've accepted is difficult.

The content for a thank-you e-mail need not differ much, if at all, from that of a paper thank-you letter (see the preceding section). You can write a couple of lines in your e-mail referring to your attached letter:

I was impressed with the warmth and efficiency of your offices, as I explain in my attached letter.

Or you can enclose the letter's content within the body of your e-mail if plain text is satisfactory.

Telephone calls

Once upon a time, all that job seekers had to worry about when calling about potential employment was getting past gatekeepers. They solved that problem in various ways, by adopting a pleasant and honest manner and making an ally of the assistant by revealing the refreshing truth about why they're calling, as one example. Some job seekers battled back by trying to reach the interviewer before 8:30 a.m. or after 5:30 p.m., when the assistant wasn't likely to be on deck and the interviewer alone would pick up the phone.

Those were the good old days. Now voicemail has joined gatekeepers in throwing 800-pound roadblocks in front of job seekers who try to follow up on interviews.

The big voicemail question for job seekers is whether to leave a message on voicemail. Opinions vary, but, as a practical matter, you may have to leave a message if you don't connect after the first few calls. All your calls won't be returned, but your chances improve when you say something interesting in a 30-second sound bite:

> *This is _____. I'm calling about the (job title or department) opening. After reflecting on some of the issues you mentioned during our meeting, I thought of a solution for one problem you might like to know. My number is _____.*

If you do manage to catch the interviewer by phone, it helps to have a thoughtful way of opening the conversation. Here's a sprinkling of conversation starters:

> *Is this a good time to talk?*
>
> *I think you'll be interested to know _____.*
>
> *I understand you're still reviewing many applications, but. . . .*
>
> *I forgot to go into the key details of (something mentioned during the interview) that may be important to you.*
>
> *While listening to you, I neglected to mention my experience in (function). It was too important for me to leave out, since the position calls for substantial background in that area.*
>
> *I was impressed with your _____.*
>
> *I appreciate your emphasis on _____.*

After the interviewer is engaged, try these approaches to keep the conversational ball rolling:

- ✔ Remind the interviewer of why you're so special and what makes you unique (exceptional work in a specific situation, innovating).

  Let me review what I'm offering you that's special.

- ✔ Establish a common denominator — a work or business philosophy.

  It seems like we both approach work in the (name of) industry from the same angle.

- ✔ Note a shared interest that benefits the employer.

I found a new website that may interest you — it's XYZ. It reports on the news items we discussed. . . . Would you like the URL?

Your After-Interview Checklist

Experts in any field become experts because they've made more mistakes than the rest of us. After your interview, take a few minutes to rate how well you did. The following checklist can help you curb bad habits and become an expert at job interviewing:

✔ Were you on time?

✔ Did you use storytelling, examples, results, and measurement of achievements to back up your claims and convince the questioner that you have the skills to do the job?

✔ Did you display high energy? Flexibility? Interest in learning new things?

✔ Did the opening of the interview go smoothly?

✔ Did you frequently make a strong connection between the job's requirements and your qualifications?

✔ Was your personal grooming immaculate? Were you dressed like company employees?

✔ Did you forget any important selling points? If so, did you put them in a follow-up e-mail, letter, or call-back?

✔ Did you smile? Did you make eye contact? Was your handshake good?

✔ Did you convey at least five major qualities the interviewer should remember about you?

✔ Did you make clear your understanding of the work involved in the job?

✔ Did you use enthusiasm and motivation to indicate that you're willing to do the job?

✔ Did you find some common ground to establish that you'll fit well into the company?

✔ Did you take the interviewer's clues to wrap it up?

✔ Did you find out the next step and leave the door open for your follow-up?

✔ After the interview, did you write down names and points discussed?

✔ What did you do or say that the interviewer obviously liked?

✔ Did you hijack the interview by grabbing control or speaking too much (more than half the time)?

✔ Would you have done something differently if you could redo the interview?

Feedback when you're not offered the job

Disappointed job seekers often ask interviewers for reasons why they weren't selected and for tips on how to do better in the future. Don't waste your time: You'll almost never be given the real reason.

Employers have no legal or ethical obligation to explain why you weren't the one. Instead, they're likely to offer these kinds of useless rationales: "We didn't feel you were the best fit for this job" or "We chose another candidate who had more experience" or "Company policy won't allow me to comment."

Why won't interviewers share the truth? Here are some of the reasons:

✔ **Legal exposure:** Companies are extremely wary of lawsuits accusing them of discrimination. The less said, the less to be sued about.

✔ **Fast-paced world:** There's no profit in wasting prime hours on a dead end.

✔ **Discomfort factor:** Managers dislike giving negative feedback.

✔ **Scant information:** Human resources interviewers may not have enough details from hiring managers to give helpful answers, even if they're inclined to do so.

When you're not offered the part, review the After-Interview Checklist in this chapter. If you have the requisite qualifications and your performance doesn't need pumping up, the reason you didn't get an offer may have nothing to do with you. Square your shoulders for the next interview.

Chapter 7

Be in the Know before You Go

In This Chapter

▶ Researching to open doors that keep you outside

▶ Gleaning information to soar above the competition

▶ Chasing down the right research and nailing it

*E*ven if you'd rather scrub morgue floors than do quiz-show-quality research on organizations and their people, suck it up and dig right in — or hire someone to handle the research ditch-digging for you. Consider the rewards:

✔ You'll have solid facts demonstrating harmony between your qualifications and the job's requirements.

✔ You'll grab data suggesting you're a good fit with an employer's organizational culture.

✔ You'll own ammo for brilliant answers when asked, "What do you know about our company?"

✔ You'll gain the foundation to absorb new facts during the interview.

✔ Your preparedness will encourage the interviewer to look favorably on you.

Consider this chapter your pre-interview fact-finding resource. It reveals exactly what you can find out about a company online, shares sample questions designed to quickly get you the info you need, and points you to places where you can acquire all sorts of important details.

The more responsible the job — or the more competitive the race — the greater the amount of research you must do to pull ahead of other candidates.

What Online Searches Reveal

Building a treasury of free and useful information on most public — and some private — companies is as fast and easy as following directions to "click here." In just an hour or two, you can feast your eyes on these resources:

- ✔ Annual reports
- ✔ Financial data
- ✔ News releases
- ✔ Information about products and services
- ✔ Industry trends
- ✔ Competitor information

You may also be able to find out about

- ✔ Employee views on a company
- ✔ Pending mergers and acquisitions
- ✔ Imminent layoffs
- ✔ Shifts in management personnel
- ✔ Corporate culture
- ✔ Wall Street's outlook for the company

Take a pass when you discover a company teetering on a legal edge or dumping employees despite its past promises. But when you discover no impending corporate collapse or toxic bosses running the show, and you want the job, research is a tiebreaker in a tight race with another candidate.

Using Specific Questions to Focus Your Research

To maximize benefits from the time you spend researching a company prior to an interview, it helps to create a list of questions targeted to such concerns as the company's size and growth patterns, its competitive profile, its culture and reputation, and so on. The following sections present questions you can use to guide your research.

Size and growth patterns

The size of a company and the scope of its operations say a great deal about the company's ambitions and opportunities for advancement. Try to answer the following questions:

- ✔ What is the company's industry?
- ✔ Has the company expanded globally?
- ✔ Is it expanding or downsizing?
- ✔ What are its divisions and subsidiaries?
- ✔ How many employees does it have?
- ✔ How many clients does it serve?
- ✔ How many locations does it have?
- ✔ Does it have foreign satellites?

Direction and planning

Answers to questions about the company's plans may be difficult to find outside of the company's website, its annual report, newspaper business pages, business magazines, or the industry's trade publications. The following information is worth pursuing though, because it lets you know some of the hot issues to address or avoid:

- ✔ What are the company's current priorities?
- ✔ What is its mission?
- ✔ What long-term contracts has it established?

> ✔ What are its prospects?
>
> ✔ What are its problems?
>
> ✔ Is it initiating any new products or projects?

Products or services

You don't want to go into a job interview without at least knowing what products or services form the bedrock of the company's business. Find answers to these questions about any company you pursue:

> ✔ What services or products does the company provide?
>
> ✔ What are its areas of expertise?
>
> ✔ How does it innovate in the industry — by maintaining cutting-edge products, cutting costs, or what?

Competitive profile

How the company is positioned within its industry and how hard competitors are nipping at its heels are measures of the company's long-term health and the relative stability of your prospective job there. Get to the bottom of these issues by asking these questions:

> ✔ Who are the company's competitors?
>
> ✔ What are the company's current projects?
>
> ✔ What setbacks has it experienced?
>
> ✔ What are its greatest accomplishments?
>
> ✔ Is the company in a growing industry?
>
> ✔ Will technology dim its future?
>
> ✔ Does it operate with updated technology?

Culture and reputation

How fast is the pace? Frantic? Laid-back? Formal? Informal? Aggressive? Answers to the following questions give you clues about a company's culture:

✔ Does the company run lean on staffing?

✔ What's the picture on mergers and acquisitions?

✔ What's its reputation?

✔ What types of employees does it hire?

✔ What's the buzz on its managers?

✔ How does it treat employees?

✔ Does it push out older workers?

Company financials

Collecting current and accurate information about financials is a long chase, but it's better to discover a company's shaky financial picture before you're hired than after you're laid off. Dig (deeply if you have to) for the following nuggets:

✔ What are the company's sales?

✔ What are its earnings?

✔ What are its assets?

✔ How stable is its financial base?

✔ Is its profit trend up or down?

✔ How much of its earnings go to pay employees?

✔ Is it privately or publicly owned?

✔ Is it a subsidiary or a division of a big company?

✔ How deep in debt is the company?

Ready, Aim, Fact-Find

As you begin to scope out and scoop up information for your job search, what curtains must you part?

Privately owned companies are harder to track than publicly owned companies. Local and regional companies are harder to check out than national companies. And discovering the details on a corporation's subsidiaries or divisions is more challenging than finding out about the corporation as a whole.

Ferreting out the financial and personnel scoop on small and medium-size companies — where the great majority of jobs are found — is a still greater challenge. And unpeeling the onion on start-ups is a major sleuthing gig.

Here are basic questions paired with concise answers to speed you on your way:

Q. Where can I find free guides and tutorials to research companies?

A. The Riley Guide's *How to Research Employers* offers a collection of useful resources. Find it at `www.rileyguide.com/employer.html`.

Jobstar Central is a California library-sponsored website with organized research leads that are useful almost anywhere in the United States. Find it at `jobstar.org/hidden/coinfo.php`.

Q. Where can I find a variety of free information about companies?

A. Here's a sampling of available research that's not too hard to prospect:

- Company websites are the best place to begin. Run a Google search on the company name. Find Google at `www.google.com`.

- EDGAR is a government database that provides public access to corporate information. It allows you to quickly research a company's financial information and operations by reviewing documents filed on Forms 10-K and 10-Q with the Securities Exchange Commission. Find it at `www.sec.gov/edgar.shtml`.

- The Public Register Online (`www.annualreportservice.com`) is the largest free directory of online annual reports available on the web.

- Yahoo! Finance (`finance.yahoo.com`) publishes a wide variety of business information you may deem useful.

- Large public and college libraries with business and reference departments inventory a number of resources priced for institutions but free for your use. (College and university libraries typically restrict subscription database access to students, alumni, and faculty.) For example, Plunkett Research Online is a terrific resource for easy-to-understand analysis of trends, challenges, and opportunities in the most important industry sectors, from health care to InfoTech, from banking to energy.

- The social network LinkedIn (www.linkedin.com) allows you to find people who work at a company you're researching and ask them about it.

Q. How can I find out about smaller companies that aren't in the databases?

A. Jack Plunkett, who heads Plunkett Research Ltd. (www.plunkettresearch.com), a leading provider of business and industry information, says that most private companies won't divulge financial information to employees or to job seekers. "However, a few very entrepreneurial firms call themselves 'open companies,' meaning they let all employees know about financial results each month," Plunkett explains.

What about a company that's not "open"? Plunkett advises that you politely ask such questions as, *What's the source of the company's backing? Venture capital? Partners? Family-owned? Angel investors? Is the company profitable?* When the company is funded by venture capital or angel investors, the business research expert warns job seekers to beware of potential financial instability.

Here are further ways to get the goods when information isn't readily available:

- Search local business newspapers published by American City Business Journals. Find them at www.bizjournals.com.

- Company websites won't tell you about financial stability, but you may get clues to the company's customers and suppliers. Call and say you're doing a credit check (which is true) on the company you're investigating.

- Competitors often have a fair idea of a company's financials. Perhaps you can find someone who knows someone who knows someone.

- When you really want reassurance, go to Hoover's, Inc., (www.hoovers.com) and use its links to order a credit report on the employer. These reports, compiled by D&B or a credit bureau, can help you determine whether the company is paying its bills on time or has other problems that warn you away from accepting a job offer. The downside? The reports aren't cheap — find out the cost before ordering one.

- Suppose you're dealing with a mini company, such as one with a half-dozen employees. You can't find a shred of information written anywhere about the company. After the job offer, you may ask to speak privately with one or two employees "to get a sense of the company culture." Once alone, you can try to find out what, if anything, the employer doesn't want you to know. If you're replacing someone, ask to be put in touch with your predecessor.

- Notice the furnishings as you interview. Are you looking at cement blocks and boards for book-cases? The bare minimum in decor may be a clue to a serious operating capital problem.

Q. How can I check out a start-up company?

A. When historical data on a company doesn't exist, you can ask questions of the interviewer: *How much capital is on hand? How fast is it being spent? Is additional funding in place?*

Additionally, if you can snare a copy of the company's business plan, review it for probability of success with an accountant, investment banker, or SCORE consultant (a volunteer, free to you, of the U.S. Small Business Administration).

You also can make an informed guess about the competence of the principals of the firm by checking out the track record of the management team and financial backers. Try the free service of ZoomInfo (`www.zoominfo.com`), a people search engine. You can also check out the principles on LinkedIn (`www.linkedin.com`).

Library copies of *Standard & Poor's Industry Surveys* and *Plunkett's Industry Almanacs* are other good places to poke around.

View recruitment videos with eyes wide open

Companies are rushing to add videos picturing employees to their repertoires of recruiting tools. They often present these recruiting videos as a kind of day-in-the-life of a typical employee at ABC company. They can be very helpful when you watch for clues reflecting the people the company prefers to hire.

The videos are supposed to offer potential employees a glimpse of a company's work environment and culture. For example, a video may show employees seated in a cubicle farm. If you're an open-space type of person, you'll want to ask about the work-space assignment policy during your interview.

The workforce age mix is another inference you can draw from recruitment videos, according to Mark Mehler, a principal at CareerXroads, a recruiting technology consulting firm in Kendall Park, N.J. "Are all the people shown younger than 40? Or does a mix of age groups offer a hint that experienced professionals are encouraged to apply?" Mehler asks.

The videos offer insights on how to dress for your interview and the kind of work wardrobe you'd need in the related job. When everyone in the video is dressed in casual attire and your grooming hallmark is a business suit — or vice versa — you're probably in the wrong theater.

In an abundance of caution, you may want to watch a company's recruiting video twice. And when you see one that reminds you of an infomercial, put on your critical-thinking cap. Remember that happy talkers are chosen to appear on the company's silver screen rather than grousers who tell ugly little secrets. When you see employees shown merely talking about their jobs rather than doing their jobs at their workstations, ask yourself why.

In fact, some of those smiling faces appearing in recruitment videos may belong to human relations professionals, says Todd Raphael, editorial chief at ERE Media (www.ere.net), the leading publisher of recruiting news. Raphael notes that a video may use an unfamiliar job title rather than a familiar version. A "sourcing manager" is actually a recruiter. "You want to hear from a person doing the job you want, not a company spokesperson," he advises.

Chapter 8

Practicing for the Big Day

. . . .

In This Chapter

▶ Staring down your jitters

▶ Kicking stress with video rehearsal

▶ Making body language walk your talk

. . . .

A job interview is a stressful situation. You're trying to make a good impression, establish that you're the best choice for the position, and prove you're a fine fit for the company. That's enough to throw anyone off balance and suddenly you're a bundle of nerves

The good news is there's help for a racing pulse and tummy butterflies: Practice beforehand.

As the late great American newscaster Walter Cronkite remarked, "It's natural to have butterflies. The secret is to get them to fly in formation."

This chapter helps you figure out how to calm your nerves. It also gives you pointers on recording a practice interview, using body language to your advantage, and anticipating disruptions and silences — both of which can throw you off if you don't think ahead about how to deal with them.

Taking Steps to Calm Your Nerves

You're not alone in your nervousness. Most people — including me — start out with a case of the shakes when interviewing or making a speech. When I began giving speeches, I could feel my throat drying up as panic fried my memory banks. I knew I had to go out and orate to promote my media careers column, but doing so was not my idea of fun.

Then one day things changed. I was in Florida addressing a group of career counselors when a teacher with whom I shared a podium watched me shake my way through my remarks. The teacher, herself an accomplished speaker, took me aside after the program and delivered one of the best pieces of advice I've ever been given. The teacher explained that nervousness is caused by the fear of looking ridiculous to others. She said:

> *When you are nervous, you are focusing on yourself. Try to focus on how you are helping other people by sharing with them the knowledge you've acquired.*
>
> *You've been privileged to gather information not many people have. Think about serving others, not about yourself when you're on stage.*

Her simple words of wisdom were an epiphany, a wakeup call. Thanks, Teach, for putting my nervousness into perspective.

How can *you* use that perspective? By realizing that preparing for a job interview is not unlike preparing for a speech.

Bear in mind these three basic steps to fright-free interviewing:

1. **Memorize your basic message.**

   Get your skills and competencies, accomplishments, and other qualifications down pat. Rehearse until you're comfortable answering questions and you've practiced your basic presentation techniques. Rehearse until you know your self-marketing material cold.

2. **Personalize each self-marketing interview pitch.**

   Research each potential employer to customize your basic presentation for each job. (I tell you how to go about researching prospective companies in Chapter 7.)

3. **Spotlight your audience.**

   Focus on how your talents can benefit your audience. Don't worry about how imperfect you may appear. Making your audience the center of attention goes a long way toward writing "The End" to your nervousness.

If that's not enough to put you at ease, consider the following list of suggestions:

✔ **Take deep breaths to instantly relieve stress.** Take a deep breath, breathing from your toes all the way through your body, and then slowly exhale. Repeat twice more, for three deep breaths in all.

✔ **Relax your shoulders and jaw by releasing your hands.** Clench your fists and hold for three to five seconds. Release. Repeat this process three times.

✔ **Push away anxiety.** Go into a nearby restroom and lean into a wall like a suspect being frisked in a cop show. Push hard, as though you want to push the wall down. Grunt as you push. Speech coaches say that when you push a wall and grunt, you contract certain muscles, which, in turn, reduces anxiety. Don't let anyone see you do this exercise, though — an observer may think you're loony tunes.

✔ **Visualize the outcome you want.** Top athletes often use visualization techniques to calm jitters, improve concentration, and boost athletic performance. They picture in their mind opponents' actions and strategy, and then picture themselves countering the maneuver. For an interview, you can visualize meeting the interviewer, answering and asking questions, and closing the interview well.

✔ **Combine relaxation with visualization.** Visualize a quiet, beautiful scene, such as a green valley filled with wildflowers or a soothing garden with a waterfall. Inhale and think, "I am." Exhale and think, "Calm." Breathe at least 12 times. Next, recall a successful interview experience.

Rehearsing out loud

Practice speaking aloud the messages you plan to deliver at your job interview — such as a listing of your five top skills, how you'll answer questions (see Chapter 4 for tips), and how you'll ask questions (flip to Chapter 5 for ideas).

Why not just silently read your message statements over and over? Coaching experts say *rehearsing* information helps fix content in your mind. Rehearsing your statements at least five times makes them yours.

Before an interview, free your mind of personal worries — like paying the mortgage or picking up your kid after school. When your personal concerns can't be handled immediately — and most can't — write them down and promise yourself that you'll deal with them after your job interview.

Practicing with a Video Recorder

Discover yourself through an employer's eyes. With a friend feeding you expected questions, practice your interview answers using a video-recording device. These devices range from computer-connected video cams with microphones and smartphones with recording software, to camcorders that both record and play back, to full-blown theater systems.

You don't have to rush out and buy some gee-whiz new technology. Use whatever device is available to you that will record and play back an hour-long picture and audio. Your performance is the message, not the system you use to make it happen.

Recording a practice session enables you to see how — with image improvement and mannerism modification — you can look alert, competent, and confident. You can refine actions that turn on hiring action and eliminate those that turn off hiring action. Rehearse nonverbal as well as spoken messages and keep an eye out for the following image-detracting actions:

- Leg swinging
- Foot tapping
- Rocking from side to side
- Fiddling with your hair
- Waving around nervous hands
- Leaning back
- Crossing your arms
- Bowing your head frequently
- Darting your eyes

✔ Blinking slowly (comes across as disinterest or slow thinking)

✔ Touching your mouth constantly

✔ Forgetting to smile

Use the following techniques to put your readiest foot forward:

✔ Pause and think before answering a question to seem thoughtful and unflappable.

✔ Refer to your notes, and you're seen as one who covers all the bases. Just don't make the mistake of holding on to your notes like they're a life preserver.

✔ If you find your voice sounds tight and creaky on tape, try warming up before an interview or your next practice run: Sing in the shower or in your car on the way to the interview. La la la la. . . . Maybe you shouldn't sing on the bus.

Unlocking the Power of Body Language

Carol Kinsey Goman (www.ckg.com) is one of the business world's foremost authorities on body language. An executive coach, popular author, and keynote speaker, Dr. Goman explains a phenomenon that you probably haven't thought much about: In a job interview, two conversations are going on at the same time. The second conversation, the nonverbal one, can seriously support or disastrously weaken your spoken words.

Fascinated, on behalf of job seekers everywhere, I interviewed Dr. Goman. Here are my questions, followed by Dr. Goman's answers:

How quickly does body language impact your interview?

Immediately! Starting with the first steps you take inside the interviewing room, interviewers make judgments about you within seconds. The precise number of seconds is debated by social psychologists and interviewing professionals — it's complicated.

But most researchers and first-impression observers agree that initially sizing you up requires mere seconds. In that wisp of time, decisions are made about your credibility, trustworthiness, warmth, empathy, confidence, and competence.

While you can't stop people from making snap decisions — the human brain is hardwired in this way — you *can* understand how to make those decisions work in your favor.

What can you say in seconds, other than "Hello"?

Obviously, you won't impress anyone by what you say in time measured by seconds. Instead, it's all about what you *don't* say. It's all about your body language.

But if you fail to score during the first impressionable seconds, can't you recover your chances later in the interview?

A poor first impression is hard to overcome, no matter how solid your credentials or impressive your resume.

So how can you do well in an interview from the get-go?

Here are powerful ways you can make a favorable first impression:

- ✔ **Command your attitude.** People pick up your attitude instantly. Think about the situation. Make a conscious choice about the attitude you want to communicate. Attitudes that attract people are friendly, cheerful, receptive, patient, approachable, welcoming, helpful, and curious. Attitudes that deter people are angry, impatient, bored, arrogant, fearful, disheartened, and distrustful.

- ✔ **Stand tall.** Your body language is a reflection of your emotions, but it also influences your emotions. Start projecting confidence and credibility by standing up straight, pulling your shoulders back, and holding your head high. Just by assuming this physical position, you'll begin to feel surer of yourself.

- ✔ **Smile.** A smile is an invitation, a sign of welcome. It says, "I'm friendly and approachable." Smiling influences how other people respond.

  The human brain prefers happy faces, recognizing them more quickly than those with negative expressions.

Research shows that when you smile at someone, the smile activates that person's reward center. It's a natural response for the other person to smile back at you.

✔ **Make eye contact.** Looking at someone's eyes transmits energy and indicates interest and openness. A simple way to improve your eye contact in those first few seconds is to look into the interviewer's eyes long enough to notice what color they are. With this one simple technique, you'll dramatically increase your likeability factor.

If you feel uncomfortable looking into an interviewer's eyes too long, look the interviewer squarely in the nose, and you appear to be making eye contact. You communicate openness and honesty.

Although good eye contact is excellent body language, don't try for a laser lock on the interviewer. Imagine two cats in a staring contest — in the Animal Kingdom, nobody moves until somebody swats. Break the tension by periodically looking away.

✔ **Raise your eyebrows.** Open your eyes slightly more than normal to simulate the "eyebrow flash" that is the universal signal of recognition and acknowledgment.

✔ **Lean in slightly.** Leaning forward with the small of your back against the chair shows you're engaged and interested. We naturally lean toward people and things we like or agree with. But be respectful of the other person's space.

✔ **Shake hands.** This is the quickest way to establish rapport. It's also the most effective. Research confirms that it takes an average of three hours of continuous interaction to develop the same level of rapport that you can get with a single handshake.

When shaking hands, make sure you keep your body squared off to the other person, facing the person fully. Use a firm — but not bone-crushing — grip with palm-to-palm contact. And hold the other person's hand a few fractions of a second longer than you're naturally inclined to do. This action conveys additional sincerity and quite literally "holds" the other person's attention while you exchange greetings.

What are some of the top flops in body language?

Avoid doing the following, all of which indicate nervousness, submission, or weakness:

- ✔ **Projecting agitation:** Try not to fidget or change positions frequently. Don't bounce your legs, lock your ankles, or rock from side to side. Don't dart your eyes, blink in slow motion, or blink abnormally fast. Never wave your arms with hands over your head to make a point because it implies that you're out of control.

- ✔ **Looking disinterested:** Overcome any tendency to cross your arms, which suggests disagreement or disbelief, especially when leaning back. Avoid continually bowing your head, as though you're saying, "I have no idea of the right answer" or "Poor me."

- ✔ **Seeming unsure:** Standing with your feet close together can make you seem timid. (Widen your stance, relax your knees, and center your weight in your lower body to look more "solid" and sure of yourself.) Avoid hanging on to your laptop, purse, or briefcase as though it's Linus's security blanket in the Charlie Brown comics.

- ✔ **Appearing tired:** Slumping in the chair is a really bad idea. "Slacker" is the first thing that comes to mind if you're a member of the Gen Y generation, and "old timer" arises if you're a boomer.

- ✔ **Suggesting arrogance:** A nonverbal signal of confidence is holding your head up. But if you tilt your head back even slightly, the signal changes to one of looking down your nose at the interviewer or job being discussed.

Different strokes for different folks

When you're applying for certain types of jobs, your tone of voice or head position may make all the difference in winning the gig. For example, when you're going for a

- ✔ **Service job:** You'll seem more personable by slightly tilting up your chin and letting your voice rise by a hair at the end of each key sentence.

- ✔ **Management job:** You'll come across as more boss-like by using a steady, calm, and confident voice as you keep your chin level.

Make Like an A-List Candidate

As you rehearse your interviewing presentation, aim for the A-list of candidates by heeding the following hints:

✔ Practice focusing your discussion on the employer's needs. Show that you understand those needs, that you possess the specific skills to handle the job, and that you're in sync with the company culture.

✔ Don't discuss previous employment rejections — unless you want to come off as a constant reject.

✔ Develop and practice justifiably proud statements of your accomplishments — that is, those that directly relate to the job you want.

✔ Practice descriptions of your leadership qualities and initiative and remember to express them *in context* of what you accomplished. (Did you lead 10 people, 100 people, or 1,000 people? What was the result? Has anyone in the company accomplished the same thing?)

✔ Be willing to admit a misstep. If pressed, you can 'fess up to a goof you've made in your career (when was it — 3:48 p.m. on June 14, 2011?). But rehearse satisfying explanations of how you learned from your one mistake — or two or three. And try not to laugh while you're admitting that you're human.

Anticipating Interview Trapdoors

No matter how well you're doing as you sail through an interview, certain things can throw you off balance when you're not forewarned. Rehearse in your mind how you would handle the situations in the upcoming sections.

Disruptions

As you rehearse, keep in mind that not everything that happens during the interview is related to you. Your meeting may be interrupted by a ringing phone, the interviewer's co-workers, or even the interviewer's emergency needs. Add the factor of interview interference to your mock drills.

Because the show must go on, find language to politely over-look these interruptions with patient concentration. Practice keeping a tab on what you're discussing between disruptions, in case the interviewer doesn't.

Silent treatment

Interviewers sometimes use silence strategically. Moments of silence are intended to get candidates to answer questions more fully — and even to get them to blurt out harmful infor-mation they had no intention of revealing.

Instead of concentrating on your discomfort during silences, recognize the technique. Either wait out the silence until the interviewer speaks or fill it with a well-chosen question that you have tucked up your sleeve (like the ones in Chapter 5). Don't bite on the silent treatment ploy, panic, and spill infor-mation that doesn't advance your cause.

Turning the tables, you can use your own silence strategy to encourage the interviewer to elaborate or to show that you're carefully considering issues under discussion.

Chapter 9

Dressing the Part

. . . .

In This Chapter

▶ Recognizing what message you send with your interview attire

▶ Minding the number one commandment of interview dressing

▶ Surveying conservative versus business casual attire

. . . .

The clothes on your back are the tip-off to the line of work you're in. Any observer over the age of 5 knows that Lady Gaga is an entertainer, not a firefighter or a police officer.

Sports team members wear their own color-coded costumes, physicians favor white coats, and priests don clerical clothing. Bankers dress to impress in hand-tailored dress suits, and hazmat technicians dress to survive in chemical coveralls.

When you want to launch your career — or take it up a notch, or pull it back from the edge — you need the right attire for your job interviews. You want your clothes, accessories, and grooming to make a smash-hit first impression because first impressions strongly impact the entire interview. This chapter details how to impress the hiring squad by selecting interviewing attire that boosts your confidence.

You Are What You Wear

"Send a message through your clothing and be aware of the details" is solid advice from international business dress expert Barbara Pachter, who lectures, consults, and writes on the topic.

So what are the wrong messages to send? Pachter (www.pachter.com) cuts to the chase, naming eight succinct knock-out punches you don't want your outfit to deliver at job interviews:

- ✔ **Wearing clothes that are too big:** You'll look like a little kid in your big brother or sister's clothing! Your clothing needs to fit.

- ✔ **Wearing skirts that are too short:** A short skirt draws attention to legs. Is that where you want people to look?

- ✔ **Showing cleavage:** Sexy isn't a corporate look. Low-cut tops that expose cleavage draw attention to this body part and aren't appropriate in the office.

- ✔ **Wearing short socks:** Socks that fall down expose skin and hairy legs when men sit or cross their legs.

- ✔ **Using color to draw attention to your clothing:** Do you want to be remembered for what you said or what you wore? A man wearing bright green slacks, which aren't typical corporate clothing, would probably be labeled as "the man in green pants."

- ✔ **Wearing clothing with inappropriate messaging or design:** A candidate wearing a shirt with small teddy bears won't get the job — his interviewers will just be talking about his shirt.

- ✔ **Forgetting about your shoes:** People notice shoes. Your shoes must be clean, polished, and in good condition.

- ✔ **Ignoring your grooming:** Your clothes need to be clean and pressed. No safety pins for buttons. No holes. No frays. No chipped nail polish. No nose hairs. They become distractions that lead to no job offer.

Dressing to Fit the Job and the Job's Culture

By choosing attire that's appropriate to the position you're aiming for and the employer's culture, you're sending the signal that you respect the company's culture and that you care enough to expend the effort to make the right impression.

Social DNA draws people to others who are like them. When extending a warm welcome to a newcomer, you pay compliments that communicate the message "You're one of us."

When you look the part, the part plays itself

A retired recruiter, Jack D. Stewart of Abilene, Texas, once accepted a recruiting search for an industrial sales rep. The job order came from a new client. Stewart's firm began referring quality candidates, recommending to the candidates that they dress conservatively for their interviews, meaning business suits, well-pressed shirts, and silk ties.

Six interviews with different individuals brought the same puzzling response from the new client: "Each candidate was basically qualified, but not what we're looking for."

Stewart's firm had a policy of reevaluating a client's assignment when six candidates were referred and none received a job offer. A recruiter was sent to the client's offices to uncover the problem.

Imagine the recruiter's astonishment when he entered an office filled with people dressed in very casual slacks and sport shirts sans ties. "Well," the recruiter thought, "these must be the foot soldiers. What does the captain wear?" The recruiter found out soon enough when the sales manager arrived to greet him in a pair of black work shoes topped by white socks.

"From that day forward," Stewart explains, "we dressed down our candidates for their interviews with that client — but we couldn't bring ourselves to tell them to wear white socks. Finally, one of our referrals was hired. The experience is a good reminder for job interviewees: *When in Rome, wear a toga.*"

Companies and organizations are made of people working as a group to accomplish common goals. An anthropologist may think of such a group as a kind of workplace tribe.

When your choice of clothing or your grooming keeps you from looking as though you're a member of the tribe, you create an image of an outsider, perhaps causing the interviewer to perceive you as "not one of us." So if you really want the job, make the effort to look as though you absolutely belong on the company's tribal land.

How can you find out about the company's dress code and grooming conventions? You have several options:

> ✔ Visit the company's website and search for videos of employees. *Pay attention to how employees dress at the level of position you seek — clerk, manager, or executive.*
>
> ✔ Call the human resources office and ask about the company's dress code.
>
> ✔ Use your personal network — or an online social network — to find an employee whom you can quiz.
>
> ✔ Loiter near the workplace and observe employees coming and going. Check for beards, mustaches, and long, loose hair. Notice whether the men are wearing sport jackets or suits, or simply shirts with or without a tie. Observe whether the women are in pants or skirts.

Correctly interpreting the company dress code is the number one commandment to follow in dressing for job interviews.

Selecting from the Basic Types of Interview Wardrobes

Both women and men should expect every nuance of their appearance to be noted and interpreted at a job interview. As Mark Twain supposedly said, "Clothes make the man. Naked people have little or no influence on society."

When you're getting ready for the big days, choose your attire from these four basic fashion categories:

> ✔ **Conservative:** Examples of conservative dressing environments include banks, law offices, accounting firms, and management offices — especially in big corporations.
>
> ✔ **Business casual:** Business-casual environments and career fields include information technology, sales, government agencies, education, retail, real estate, engineering, small companies, and Internet firms. (*Smart casual* — a term sometimes interchangeably used with *business casual* — means a loosely defined but pulled-together informal look for both men and women.)
>
> ✔ **Casual:** Plain casual environments are those such as construction, trucking, maintenance, repair, landscaping, and

other jobs where work clothes may end the day stained and sweaty.

✔ **Creative fashion:** Clothing worn in career fields such as entertainment, fashion, graphic design, interior design, popular music, and other arts.

I tell you more about each category in the sections that follow.

Remaining conservative

Conservative dressing means no surprises. Your look is traditional or restrained in style. You avoid showiness. You aren't flamboyant. Conservative dressing means you not only wear the established team uniform, but you wear it well, from the tip of your white collar to the closed toe of your dark shoes.

For *women,* a conservative checklist includes the following:

✔ **Suit:** Wear a two-piece suit or a simple dress with a jacket. Good colors are navy blue, gray, dark green, dark red, burgundy, and black. Make sure your skirt length is a bit below the knee or not shorter than just above the knee.

In a dark color, a pantsuit is a tasteful choice. Accessorize it with a simple shell and silk scarf. *Caveat:* If your research shows you're interviewing with a super-traditionalist, stick to skirts.

✔ **Shirt:** A white, off-white, or neutral-colored blouse is a safe choice.

✔ **Shoes:** Closed-toe pumps with low heels or midheels (2½ to 3½ inches) suggest that you're work-minded.

✔ **Accessories:** Briefcases look more serious than purses, but a handsome leather purse is fine. Avoid distracting jewelry or watches.

✔ **Makeup:** Moderate makeup for daytime wear is appropriate. No looking like a cast member of *Jersey Shore.*

✔ **Hair:** Simply styled hair looks contemporary; observe styles on TV anchors, for whom maintaining a professional image is essential.

For *men,* the following conservative checklist applies:

- ✔ **Suit:** Power-suit colors are navy or charcoal gray. (Black on men is seen as somber.) Tans and medium-tone colors work well if your research shows they're included in the company's color chart for team uniforms. Suits should be well tailored.

- ✔ **Shirt:** White is the first choice for shirts; blue is second. In either case, wear only long sleeves.

- ✔ **Tie:** Dark or low-key (blue, black, navy, or gray) or power-red colors bring to mind executives. Geometric patterns are okay, but only if they're minimal. Be sure your necktie knot is neat and centered on your neck; the bottom of the tie should just reach your belt. Skip the bowtie.

- ✔ **Shoes:** Wear lace-up shoes in the same color as your belt. Wear black shoes if your suit is gray or navy; wear dark brown shoes for tans or medium-tone colors — in both cases, choose polished and clean shoes that are in good condition. Rubber-soled shoes are a bad match for a professional suit and tie, as are alligator shoes or sandals.

- ✔ **Socks:** Wear dark socks in midcalf length so no skin shows when you sit down.

- ✔ **Accessories:** Limit jewelry to a wristwatch and, if you wear them, cufflinks.

Cruising business casual

An increasing number of recruiters say that a business suit is too formal for an interview at their company. Enter business casual attire. The interpretation of *business casual* varies too widely for universally accepted rules, but mainstream opinion nixes casual clothing you'd wear to a picnic or a ballgame, such as sweat suits, spandex, shorts, T-shirts with slogans or commercial logos, bare midriffs, halter tops, and tank tops.

About that fragrance

Perfumes and after-shave scents should be minimal or missing. A number of people are allergic; others may be reminded by the fragrance of someone they didn't enjoy knowing.

Oh pantyhose, oh pantyhose, wherefore art thou pantyhose?

If you think the issue of tats and bling on the interview stage is a touchy subject, reflect on the issue of bare-legged ladies.

Opinions on both sides of the generational divide could start a new rumble in a Shakespearean tale of feuding noble families. Regardless of the weather or locale, younger women say that wearing pantyhose is silly, while their elders huff that not wearing pantyhose is tacky.

Professional presence guru Barbara Pachter makes two excellent points for women on how to handle the dilemma:

✔ When you wear pants or a pantsuit, your legs aren't exposed, and the issue of whether to wear hose becomes moot.

✔ When your legs have blemishes, scars, or varicose veins, pantyhose diminishes their unattractive appearance.

Dress code research before an interview gives you a leg up on the pantyhose predicament.

For *women*, a business casual checklist includes the following:

✔ **Clothing:** Guidelines here are looser than for conservative dress. Sticking with the following points is a safe bet:

- A casual jacket or blazer with well-pressed trousers or a skirt is a top option.

- A jacketed tailored dress is a fine choice.

- Tailored knit sweaters and sweater sets are appropriate.

- A skirt that's knee length, or longer, paired with a blouse works well for support jobs.

- Avoid pastel overload (pink, baby blue); those colors work great for a nursery but not for your professional outfit.

- Provocative clothing (see-through tops, uncovered cleavage, second-skin pants, shimmering fabric, super-short skirts) isn't your best look for attracting offers at the top of the salary scale.

✔ **Shoes:** Shoes should look businesslike and be dark colored — no strappy shoes, sandals, or mile-high stilettos.

✔ **Makeup:** Avoid wearing heavy makeup — on you or on your collar line.

✔ **Accessories:** Leave flashy or distracting jewelry — dangly ding-a-ling earrings, clunky bracelets, giant spiky rings that bruise fingers when shaking hands — at home in your jewelry box. And avoid chipped nail polish, if you wear it.

For *men,* a business casual checklist includes the following:

✔ **Clothing:** Don a sport jacket or blazer, especially navy blue, black, or gray, with color-coordinated long trousers or pressed khakis. Shirts should have collars, be long sleeved, and stay tucked into pants; button-down shirts are good but not mandatory.

✔ **Shoes:** Choose dress shoes and a matching belt; loafers are acceptable.

✔ **Socks:** Wear dark socks that are midcalf length.

✔ **Ties:** Choose simple (not too busy) ties for job interviews, unless you know from your research that a tie isn't part of the uniform where you're interviewing.

✔ **Accessories:** Limit jewelry to a conservative wristwatch.

Nail polish gone wild

Should you sport any nail color other than the classic reds and pinks at a job interview? How about blue, green, orange, purple, or turquoise nail polish? So many women apply wild nail colors that this color celebration once thought to be a passing fad has moved into mainstream acceptance. Good idea? Bad idea? Career coaches' opinions vary.

The "No" answer: Stick with conservative colors in case the hiring decider is a fuddy-duddy who hates trying new things or who considers the unconventional end of the color palette to be in vulgar taste.

The "Yes" answer: Ditch the sparkles and yard-long nails, but don't leave wild colors to tweens, teens, and twenty-somethings. Become an early adopter because it suggests that you lean forward to stay up with the times — a good strategy for the more mature set.

Don't let them smell you first

Grooming has a strong influence on hiring decisions. Who hasn't nearly passed out after smelling someone's salami breath? Who hasn't been revolted by rank body odor? Who hasn't been turned off by spinach flecks on teeth?

A recent National Association of Colleges and Employers survey reports a rejection of candidates who don't pass the sniff test. In fact, 73 percent of respondents stated they don't want slovenly, smelly, or dirt-ridden employees working anywhere on the premises.

Translation: Shower. Brush. Comb. Clean is as clean smells.

Any interviewee, male or female, going for a position at a business casual company is better off steering clear of the following:

- ✔ Dark-tinted glasses and sunglasses atop your head or hanging in front of your collar
- ✔ Electronic devices (even on vibrate mode — the buzzing sound is annoying)
- ✔ Joke watches or fad watches

Advance research is the only way to be on sure footing. You're gambling if you assume that you know what business casual means in your interview setting — or even whether you should dress in business casual. When in doubt, scout it out.

Working in casual wear

True casual work attire is suitable for hands-on working men and women. Often a company uniform is required when you're on the job, but when you're in job interview mode, the main point to remember is to look neat and clean, with no holes or tears in your clothing. Colors and style don't matter as much as they do in conservative and business casual interview dressing, but your overall appearance does.

Here's a short checklist for both men and women:

- ✔ **Clothing:** Shirts or knit tops and well-pressed pants are appropriate. Avoid wrinkled or soiled clothing, and don't wear T-shirts with writing on them.

- ✔ **Shoes:** Polished leather shoes or rubber-soled athletic shoes are fine. Just don't embarrass yourself by waltzing in wearing grungy sneakers.

- ✔ **Grooming:** Make 100-percent sure your hair and fingernails are neat and clean.

Selecting creative fashion

Most job seekers interview in attire suggesting that they're serious and centered in a business culture. But if you work in a creative environment, take fashion risks and go for artistry, design consciousness, innovation, trendiness, new styles, and, yes, even whimsy.

You're probably way ahead of me and already follow high- and low-fashion statements online and in magazines such as *Vogue* and *Marie Claire, GQ* and *Details.* You know what they say about fashion: in one year and out the other. So I don't attempt to compile a checklist for either sex, because in a fashion-forward office, everything would be outdated by the time this book is published.

Online wardrobe mistresses and masters

Fashion-focused websites are the perfect media to track the latest fashion scene (what's hot and what's not seems to change every 15 minutes). For starters, try these sites:

- ✔ **Fashion.About.com** (www. fashion.about.com): A guide to women's fashion, including fashion trends

- ✔ **MensFashion.About.com** (www. mensfashion.about.com): A men's fashion and grooming guide for today and tomorrow

- ✔ **Ask Andy About Clothes** (www. askandyaboutclothes. com): A popular and comprehensive site devoted to men's wear that includes a feature enabling you to ask questions of an expert

Should you dress 10 percent above your level?

When you go job interviewing, the classic advice is, "Dress one step up from what you'd typically wear to work in that position." Other lines you may hear are "Dress 10 percent better than you ordinarily would" or "Dress for the position you'd like to have one day, so you'll be seen as promotable."

My take on upscaling for interview days is to "Dress the best you're ever going to look in the job you're competing for."

In offices where employees are encouraged to show originality, a reasonably creative look (not too far over the top) beats out conservative dress, and maybe business casual as well. It all depends on the company culture as seen through the hiring boss's eyes.

Chapter 10

Welcome to the 21st Century Video Interview

In This Chapter

▶ Identifying three digital roads to video face-time

▶ Prepping for your close-up video interview

*A*s smaller recruiting staffs face larger numbers of job applications, employers are turning to video interviews to cut costs when identifying viable candidates.

Overall, video technology is still most often used for initial screening, as described in Chapter 2, or for distance meet-ups when the cost of travel is prohibitive. But for lower-level jobs — such as internships, commodity jobs, and some technical positions — the online job video may be the entire interviewing package.

The 21st century transition of the job interviewing process to video screens — one that's evolving minute by minute — adds a whole new layer of techniques you'll want to master for successful job hunting.

This chapter describes the essentials of nailing the video interview, whether it's used for screening or selection.

Getting Familiar with the Three Basic Models

When you're targeting a managerial or professional job, an offer is unlikely to be extended until you and the person with hiring authority have gone nose-to-nose in the same room.

The video look-over, which may include multiple screening interviews, is usually aimed at reducing in-person meetings to a single event. Having said that, remember that nothing is fixed in bronze in today's rapidly developing online video interviewing industry. After a round of phone and video interviews, job offers are occasionally extended to candidates who've never set foot inside the employer's office.

Not all video interviewing models are the same, and some employers may use more than one model. Regardless of the model, interviewing skills are front and center in a video version. The following sections describe the three basic video interview models.

Working with third-party vendors

Private video interviewing firms such as HireVue, the first company of its kind, are fast climbing the pop charts of talent-management technology. Launched with a single Salt Lake City office in 2004, the video interviewing industry is estimated to number more than two dozen vendors in 2012. (Check out www.talentmanagementtechnologymegalist.com.)

Here's how it works: The typical method is for a third-party vendor to send the job applicant a webcam, with detailed directions on how to use it. Additionally, the vendor's website usually has detailed instructions, an 800-number to call if there are problems, and sample interviews.

Assuming you're the job seeker, after you receive an interview invitation, you log in to a server to get the interview questions, which appear on your computer screen or are spoken by an announcer or company spokesperson. You have about 30 seconds to read each question and a given amount of time (usually two to three minutes) to answer on camera.

After your interview begins, there's no turning back. The interview is recorded, and you can't edit your answers, even if you quickly realize you gave a mother-of-all-jokers answer. The questions keep coming — usually about seven to ten of them. For instance, "Can you give an example of why your past work history qualifies you for this position?"

Chatting through Skype

You can interview live using Skype, an online phone and video Internet service. But you need a computer, a webcam, and a decent broadband connection.

Skype started in 2003, and its name is short for "sky peer-to-peer." Free to use in its basic version, with an easy registration process, Skype is the best-known service of its type. Skype is now the preferred method many employers use to conduct long-distance screening interviews, although a number stick to "old-fashioned" phone screeners for simplicity. Comments by interviewees who've tried video chat interviewing range from enthusiastic to grumbly:

> *I really liked the video interview a lot better than the phone-based interview — it was a much friendlier and warmer exchange.*

> *A webcam isn't the most flattering piece of technology. It can make you look as attractive as Jason in "Friday the 13th."*

Before you make your first screen appearance on the interview scene via video chat on Skype, do the following:

✔ Download the Skype software a week or two in advance and cultivate a first-name basis with it. Set up practice training calls with your friends so you'll look comfortable and polished when real interviews come your way.

✔ Create a professional username; this isn't the scene to joke around.

✔ On the morning of a real interview, conduct a quick test of the technology to ensure that your camera and microphone are working like a charm.

Videoconferencing services

Videoconferencing is conducting a conference between two or more participants at different sites by using computer networks to send audio and video data.

A two-person videoconferencing system works much like a video telephone. Each participant has a video camera, microphone, and speakers mounted on a computer. Similar to video chatting, as the two participants speak to one another, their voices are carried over the network and delivered to the other's speakers, and whatever images appear in front of the video camera appear in a window on the other participant's monitor.

Some videoconferencing services invite job candidates into an office, college career center, or other permanent setting and may utilize traditional high-end equipment.

The development of multipoint videoconferencing technology allows three or more participants to sit in a virtual conference room and talk as if they're sitting next to each other.

Rocking the Video Job Interview

The *content* of a video interview is much the same as an in-person interview. But the *execution* differs. Consider these sample reactions:

- ✔ A candidate, a cool twenty-something manager who isn't easily thrown off center, told a magazine that his video interview was "kind of nerve-wracking" and a totally different feeling from sitting in front of someone for a live interview.

- ✔ An employer reported on a comments board that a lot of things don't come across the camera and that certain factors are accentuated: "Posture, dress, comfort with uncertainty, facility with technology — all those things get highlighted and bolded during a web interview."

 Online, you can't use handshakes and ingratiating small talk as you enter and leave an interviewer's office to help imprint favorable memories of you. To compensate, include a memorable statement — a sound bite. Somewhere near the end of the interview, an experienced candidate says something like this:

> *Of the many things I've accomplished in my career, (name a top achievement) stands out as the most significant. Do you see a strong connection between my favorite accomplishment and what it will take to be very successful in this position?*

Getting ready to video interview

As with all interviews, don't walk in cold and sit down before a camera unprepared. The following suggestions brief you on what you need to know:

- ✔ **Time limits:** Find out whether you're on a clock for the interview. If the interview is scheduled for 30 minutes, consider it a rigid cut-off and don't plan on overtime.

- ✔ **Advance work:** Send materials for show-and-tell in advance of the interview, in case the interviewer wants to ask questions about an updated resume or project; you can't slide materials through the screen.

- ✔ **Content review:** Review potential questions that you're likely to be asked (see Chapter 4). Be ready to relate your qualifications to the job's requirements. Memorize examples of accomplishments that illustrate what you can bring to the company.

- ✔ **Note taking:** The jury's still out about whether you should take a notebook to video interviews and jot down points that will help you respond with clarity. I vote with the note-taking school. I think it's okay to refer to your notes (and resume) and hopefully be seen as a thorough person who covers all the bases.

- ✔ **Technical check:** When you're not interviewing at home, arrive 15 to 30 minutes early at the interview site to deal with any technical issues that may arise. Request an overview of the interviewing event and a refresher on the use of the equipment. Ask the technician how loudly you should speak into the mike and how to use the picture-in-picture feature that shows you in action.

  When you're using your own video equipment, check your camera angle (set it at eye level) and speakers (place them out of view). Improve the quality of the audio by wearing a lavalier microphone clipped to your collar or tie rather than relying on the uncertain audio quality of your webcam.

Each morning before a real interview, double-check your Internet connections. Arrange to keep the other Internet traffic to a minimum during Skype sessions; make sure no one is surfing, playing online games, or watching streaming video in another room (these all compromise the bandwidth you need for Skype).

✔ **Appearance:** You can't go wrong with solid colors that aren't too dark (black) or too light (white, yellow). Blue works well. As for patterns, stick with stripes and plaids. (Busy patterns distract from your face.) See Chapter 9 for advice on what to wear for interviewing.

✔ **Background:** Plan for an uncluttered look. Eliminate such distractions as too many books or magazines, wall hangings, memos taped to the wall, stacks of laundry, posters from your favorite band, and so forth. Also, avoid background motion — think second hands ticking on a clock, barking dogs racing back and forth, cats leaping into camera range, or kids walking in and out of camera range.

✔ **Lighting:** Eliminate any bright light (as from a window) behind you — it will darken your face.

✔ **Dress rehearsal:** Arrange test interviews with friends. Can you hear each other? Can you see each other? Is the framing of your screen about right (head to waist), or is the focus on your face so tight that every pore looks like a moon crater?

Another way to prepare for a video interview is to record your performance to see for yourself how you're coming across on camera. In addition to paying attention to the quality of your answers and how you look overall, be on the lookout for awkward or off-putting behaviors. (I list several to watch out for in Chapter 8.)

During the interview

You're almost prepared to command the screen. Now review these finer points gleaned from others who have gone in front of the cameras before you.

Movements and posture

Calmness is classy and shows confidence. No way should you check your personality at the door, but do try to be fairly still. Smooooth. Avoid overly broad gestures — you're not directing traffic. Ration your gestures to underscore important information.

Pause and think before answering a question, to seem thoughtful and unflappable.

Look interested when you're seated by leaning slightly forward with the small of your back against your chair.

Microphones have an irritating habit of picking up all the noise in the room, so don't shuffle papers or tap a pen. Noises that you may not notice in a same-room interview can become annoying in a video interview.

Occasionally glance at the picture-in-picture feature on the monitor to check your body language and hope you don't catch yourself scratching, licking your lips, or jangling your keys. Hunching your shoulders and other bad-posture poses make you look even worse on those small screens than they do in person.

Facial expressions and speaking

The first thing you say is, "Hi, I'm Bill Kennedy. Nice to meet you." (And if you're not Bill Kennedy, use your own name.) Speak normally, but not too fast. When nervous, some people don't stop for air, and their best lines are left on the cutting room floor, unheard or not understood.

Be conscious of a sound delay. A couple seconds will lapse between when the interviewer speaks and when you hear the statement or question (you observe this audio pause on TV when a foreign correspondent is on another continent). At the end of an interviewer's words, pause *(One-Mississippi Moment)* before you reply.

Look directly at the camera as often as possible when speaking — this is how you make eye contact. You can look around occasionally, but avoid rolling your eyes all over the room as though you can hardly wait to make your getaway. Also, don't look down at the desk, especially if you have a bald, shiny spot on the top of your dome.

And don't bend over a microphone either (using a lavalier microphone eliminates the temptation to make like Quasimodo). Imagine that the interviewer is sitting across the table from you.

 When it comes to your facial expressions during a video interview, the three most important things to do are (1) smile, (2) smile, and (3) smile. Have you noticed that, even when reporting disasters of nationwide proportions, TV anchor people don't always wipe the smile off their faces? Why do you suppose that is? *Smile!*

Virtual handshake

Unless your interview space is on fire, it's not your prerogative to end the interview. Always allow the interviewer to indicate when time's up.

Since at the end of a video interview you can't shake hands through a monitor, deliver a sign-off statement indicating you understand that the interview is over. You can say something as simple as "Thank you for interviewing me. I enjoyed it. Let's talk face-to-face very soon." (For other sign-off ideas, review Chapter 6.)

 To end a video interview when you're in a professional setting, push the mute button and leave the room. When you're at home, mute the mike and close the camera.

Video interviews versus video resumes

A *video resume* is an employer's first look at a specific job seeker. It typically lasts between one and three minutes. The job seeker controls the content and pays for the video's production costs.

A *video interview* is an employer's second look at a specific job seeker that ordinarily takes place only by invitation after the employer evaluates the applicant's fixed online or on-paper resume. A video interview may replace a phone screening interview prior to an invitation for an on-site interview. The duration of a video interview varies. The employer controls its content and pays for it.

Chapter 11

Ten Tips for Interviewing Success

*H*eading to an interview? Spare a few minutes to review these ten tricks for interviewing success, courtesy of The Job Search Guy, Joe Turner (www.jobsearchguy.com), a career coach in Phoenix, Arizona.

Make Conversation

An interview is a conversation, a series of questions and answers. So don't fall into an answers-only rut. As soon as you answer a question, try following up with a question of your own.

Also, spend time practicing your storytelling skills so you can enter any interview armed with true, prepared stories that highlight your accomplishments. Studies suggest that people remember stories better than other forms of communication. As Mark Twain, himself no slouch as a storyteller, said, "Don't say the old lady screamed — bring her on [stage] and let her scream."

Remember Your True Goal

About 90 percent of candidates don't seem to get that their purpose in an interview is to do infinitely more than ask for a job. Not you, though. You know that your goal is two-fold:

> ✔ You want to demonstrate that you're a good "fit" for the organization — like salt and pepper, bread and butter, Jon Stewart and satire.
>
> ✔ You're looking for breaking news on whether the position is really something you want to invest a chunk of your life in.

Leave the Begging to Others

Neediness is one of the all-time deal killers in the job market. Whisper in your own ear before walking in the door: "I don't need this job. I do need air, food, and water." Keep things in perspective. Sell your strengths and your ability to do the job.

Employers don't hire because they feel sorry for you; they hire because they want you to solve *their* problems.

Be a Respectful Equal in the Discussion

Generally, you want to participate in an interview as an equal, not as a subordinate of the person conducting the interview. Of course, you should still show courteous respect to the interviewer, especially if the interviewer is a general and you're a buck private.

Participating as an equal is a subtle matter of self-perception, so remind yourself of your status before the interview begins.

Show Confidence from the Get-Go

From the moment you walk into an interview room, demonstrate confidence. Your first impression makes a difference. Stand up straight, make eye contact, and offer your interviewer an enthusiastic handshake. If you don't remember names well, jot down the interviewer's name on your notepad as soon as you're seated. Ditto for any other person you're meeting with.

Avoid Ad Libbing Ad Infinitum

Although you should always do your share to keep the conversational flow going, droning on loses your audience, and telling your interviewer more than he needs to know can be fatal. Look for an easy give-and-take in your interview without coming across as a motormouth.

Limit your stories to 90 seconds (maximum!) and make sure they have a relevant point related to your topic. Stick with your rehearsed stories, your research, your adequate answers, and the questions you need to ask.

Realize the Interviewer Isn't Your New Best Friend

Don't make the mistake of being overly familiar. A good interviewer is skilled enough to put you at ease within the first ten minutes of the interview, but that doesn't mean the interviewer has become your best friend. Never let your guard down.

You're there to give and receive information about a position that you may want. From start to finish, treat every interviewing encounter as the professional business meeting that it is.

Know That Faulty Assumptions Equal Faulty Interviewing

Making a wrong guess at what your interviewer has in mind with a particular question is guaranteed to leave you looking like you don't know what you're doing. When in doubt, ask! You don't lose points in an interview for asking questions when you don't clearly understand something.

Keep Emotions out of the Interview

The interviewer may at times consciously attempt to provoke you into a temperamental outburst. Don't fall for it or take it personally. It may be only a part of an overambitious interviewing process.

When emotions enter an interview, failure follows. So no matter how stressed out you are — the car's on the fritz, the rent is due, and you recently had an argument with your significant other — put it all behind you. Be cool, calm, and collected instead of keeping your emotions in play.

Ask Questions That Show You Care Where You Go

You want to be sure you're getting the true picture of what this job is really about and whether you want it. Arrive with a list of several prepared questions about the company, the position, and the people who work there.

Ask questions that begin with "what," "how," and "why." Avoid simple "yes" or "no" questions. Take notes.

Most interviewers are unimpressed by a candidate who has no questions. They wonder whether you're disinterested, have no sense of curiosity, dim-witted — or think you already know everything.

Index

• A •

absolutes, avoiding, 30
accessories, 127, 128, 130
accomplishments
  answering questions about,
    49, 69–70
  being specific about, 28
  using, to respond to job-hopper
    objection, 9
after-interview checklist, 101–102
after-shave, 128
age
  being asked about, 87
  range/mix, at a company, 111
agency, 2
agitation, 120
alcohol, 43
American City Business Journals
  (publisher of business
  newspapers), 109
anxiety, 113–116, 146
appearance
  body language, 17, 116–120,
    141–142
  dressing for an interview, 27, 111,
    123–133, 140
applicant, 2
appointment for phone screening,
  26–27
arrest, being asked about an,
  85, 87
arrogance, 120
The Art of the Business Lunch
  (Jay), 43
Ask Andy About Clothes
  (website), 132

attire for an interview
  fitting the job culture, 124–126
  phone screening, 27
  researching, 111
  sending a message, 123–124
  video interview, 140
  wardrobe types, 126–133
attitude, 118
automated screening interview
  about, 7
  online screening questionnaire,
    25, 31–32
  via phone, 25, 29–31

• B •

background, for video
  interview, 140
behavior-based interview,
  10–11, 36–38
being yourself, 6
bill, paying the restaurant, 46
birth date, being asked about, 87
blazer, wearing a, 129, 130
body language, 17, 116–120,
  141–142
bonding techniques, 15–16, 42
boss
  answering questions about a
    difficult, 58–59
  asking questions to learn
    about, 92
brainteaser interview, 36
branding brief, 14–15, 44–45, 46
business casual dress, 126,
  128–131

• C •

candidate, 2
career coach
  definition, 2
  James, Mark S., 27
  Turner, Joe, 16, 143
career consultant, 2
career counselor, 2
career objectives, answering
    questions about, 49–50
casual dress, 126–127, 131–132
cell phone, for screening
    interview, 26
changing the topic in a directive
    interview, 39
Chapman, Jack (author)
  Negotiating Your Salary, 32
check-back phrase, 28
checklist, after-interview,
    101–102
children, being asked
    about, 87
citizenship, being asked
    about, 87
cleavage, showing, 124, 129
closed-ended question, 39
closing the interview, 93–96, 142
clothing for an interview
  fitting the job culture, 124–126
  phone screening, 27
  researching, 111
  sending a message, 123–124
  video interview, 140
  wardrobe types, 126–133
club membership, being asked
    about, 88
color of clothing, 124, 129
comment, entering in online
    screening, 31–32
communication skill, 18–19

company. *See also* researching
    companies and industries
  answering questions about
    the, 55–58
  answering questions about
    contributing to a, 65–66
  asking questions to learn
    about a, 92
  culture, 106–107, 111, 124–126
  definition, 2
  dress conventions, 124–126
company website, researching on,
    108, 126
competitive profile, researching a
    company's, 106
competitors
  answering questions about, 56
  using, to research a company, 109
complaining, 44
complimenting, 42
confessional, interviews as a, 6
confidence, 144–145
conservative dress, 126, 127–128
consistency, in a serial
    interview, 35
consulting, abuse of, 21–22
contributing to the company,
    questions about, 65–66
conventions, explained, 1
conversation
  interview as, 143
  skill, 18–19, 145
co-workers, answering questions
    about, 66–67
creative fashion, 127, 132–133
credit record, being asked about
    your, 87
criminal conviction, being asked
    about a, 85, 87
critical incident, 39
culture, company
  dressing to fit, 124–126
  researching, 106–107, 111

• D •

decision maker, 2
decision-making, answering
    questions about, 68, 69
decision-making manager, 2
delegating, answering questions
    about, 62
demotion, answering questions
    about a, 83–84
department manager, 2
direction, researching company,
    105–106
directive interview, 39
disability, being asked about a, 87
disclosing inappropriate
    information, 6
disinterest, 120
disruptions, handling, 121–122
dramatic pause, 19
dress, business casual, 126, 128–131
dress, wearing a, 129
dressing for an interview
    fitting the job culture, 124–126
    phone screening, 27
    researching, 111
    sending a message, 123–124
    video interview, 140
    wardrobe types, 126–133

• E •

eating, 43–45
EDGAR (government database), 108
education
    appropriate questions about, 87
    speaking about, 19–20
electronic devices, 131
e-mail, following up via, 98–99
employer, 2. *See also* boss;
    company; interviewer(s)

employer's needs, focusing on,
    90–92
employment gap, questions about
    an, 82–83
exaggerating, 48
experience
    answering questions about,
    64–70
    from frequent job changes, 8
exploitation, interview, 21–22
eye contact, 18, 119, 141
eyebrows, raising, 119

• F •

facial expression, 119, 141–142
fact finding, sources for company,
    107–110
failure, answering questions about,
    53–54
family, being asked about, 87
Fashion.About.com
    (website), 132
feedback when not offered
    job, 102
fidelity, company, 9
financial information, researching
    company, 107
fired, answering questions about
    being, 77–78
firing employees, answering
    questions about, 66–67
first impression, making a good,
    18, 118
fitting in, 11–12, 144. *See also*
    dressing for an interview
focusing on yourself, 114
follow-up, interview
    e-mail, 98–99
    letter, 97–98
    phone, 99–101
food, 43–45
fragrance, 128

• *G* •

glasses, tinted, 131
goal of interview, 143–144
Goman, Carol Kinsey (body language authority), 117
grooming, 124, 131, 132
group interview, 13, 34–35
group work, 53, 62–63, 67. *See* teamwork, answering questions about
growth, researching company, 105
guides and tutorials for company research, 108

• *H* •

hair, 127
handshake
  live interview, 119
  virtual, 138–139, 142
headhunter, 2
health, being asked about, 85, 87, 88
hidden objections, questions that draw out, 91–92, 94
HireVue (video interviewing firm), 136
hiring authority, 2
hiring manager, 2
hiring professional, 2
home, being asked about your, 87
home office, using for phone interviews, 27
Hoover's, Inc. (company information website), 109–110
How to Ace the Brain Teaser Interview (Kador), 36
How to Research Employers by Riley Guide (website), 108
HR (human resources) manager, 2
HR (human resources) specialist, 2

• *I* •

icons, explained, 3–4
illegal and inappropriate interview questions, 84–88
inconsistencies, questioning to find, 24
Indeed.com (website), 74
independent recruiter, 2
industry, researching an. *See* researching companies and industries
industry-related questions, answering, 55–57
information, gathering essential, 27. *See also* researching companies and industries
integrity testing, 30
intellectual property theft, 21–22
interactive selling, 94
internal recruiter, 2
interview. *See also* interview format; screening interview; *specific topics*
  abuse, 21–22
  after-interview checklist, 101–102
  closing, 93–96, 142
  concepts to get you hired, 12–16
  dressing for, 27, 111, 123–133, 140
  follow-up, 97–101
  job offer during, 99
  practicing for, 113–122
  research preparation, 12, 79, 103–111, 126
  selection, 13, 23
  starting off, 18
  tactics, basic, 17–21
  tips for the, 42, 143–146
  trends, 7–12

interview format
 automated online screening,
  31–32
 automated phone screening,
  7, 29–30
 behavior-based, 10–11, 36–38
 brainteaser, 36
 directive, 39
 group, 13, 34–35
 job fair, 46
 live phone screening, 25, 26–29
 mealtime, 43–46
 nondirective, 40
 one-to-one, 34
 serial, 35
 stress, 40–41
 video, 7, 135–142
interview questions by interview
  type, guidance on answering.
  See also questions, asking of
  interviewers; tell-me-about-
  yourself question
 behavior-based interview,
  11, 36–38
 directive interview, 39
 nondirective interview, 40
 screening interview, 24, 30
 stress interview, 41
interview questions by subject,
  guidance on answering. *See
  also* questions, asking of
  interviewers; tell-me-about-
  yourself question
 experience and qualifications,
  63–70
 frequent job changes, 8–9
 illegal and inappropriate
  questions, 84–88
 job, company, and industry,
  55–58
 salary, 16, 32, 70–75

 sexual orientation, 78–80
 skill-related, 58–63
 special situations with prior
  employment, 75–78, 80–84
 why-should-I-hire-you question,
  55, 63
interviewee, 2
interviewer(s)
 being overly familiar with, 145
 definition, 2
 modern changes in, 8
 multiple, 13, 34–35
 observing an, 20–21

• *J* •

jacket, wearing a, 129, 130
James, Mark S. (career
  coach), 27
Jay, Robin (author)
 *The Art of the Business
  Lunch,* 43
job experience, answering
  questions about, 64–70
job fair interview, 46
*Job Interviews For Dummies,
  4th Edition* (Kennedy), 4
job knowledge, answering
  questions about, 55–56
job offer during interview, 99
job seeker, 2
job-hopper objection, responses
  to, 8–9, 80–82
jobs, questions about previous
 frequent job changes, 8–9,
  80–82
 job status changes, 65
 long time in same job, 75–77
 problems faced, 59
Jobstar Central (research
  website), 108

• K •

Kador, John (author)
  How to Ace the Brain Teaser Interview, 36
Kennedy, Joyce Lain (author)
  Job Interviews For Dummies, 4th Edition, 4
  Resumes For Dummies, 6th Edition, 14

• L •

land-line phone, for screening interview, 26
language, being asked about, 87
last job, answering questions about, 67–68
leaning in, 119, 141
Lemke, James M. (technical adviser), 23
letter follow-up, 97–98
library, using to research a company, 108–109
lighting, for video interview, 140
likeablility, 15–16, 17, 42
LinkedIn (social media website), 109, 110
listening, 20–21, 28, 42
lodge membership, being asked about, 88
loyalty, company, 9
Lucht, John (recruiting authority and author), 92
lunch interview, 43–46

• M •

makeup, 127, 130
management job, body language for a, 120
mannerisms and body language, 116–120, 141–142
marital status, being asked about, 87
market value, knowing your, 74–75

marketing yourself. *See* selling yourself
mealtime interview, 43–46
meeting, pushing for an in-person, 28–29
Mehler, Mark (CareerXroads), 111
memorable, being, 16
MensFashion.About.com (website), 132
message sent through clothing, 123–124
microphone, 141, 142
military record, being asked about, 88
mirroring, 45
mission statement, answering questions about, 57–58
mistake, answering questions about a past, 68–69
money, discussing, 16, 28

• N •

nail polish, 130
name, using interviewer's, 18
national origin, being asked about, 87
neediness, 144
negativity, 18, 44
Negotiating Your Salary (Chapman), 32
nerves, calming, 113–116, 146
nondirective interview, 40
notes
  taking, 20, 42, 139
  using, 40, 117

• O •

objection
  overcoming an, in follow-up letter, 94
  overcoming the job-hopper, 8–9, 80–82
  questioning to uncover a hidden, 91–92, 94

observing an interviewer, 20–21
one-to-one interview, 34
online screening questionnaire,
    25, 31–32
open company, 109
open-ended question, 39
oral presentation skill, answering
    questions about, 60
organization, 2
organization skill, answering
    questions about, 61
organizational membership, being
    asked about, 88

• *P* •

pace, speaking, 28
Pachter, Barbara (business attire
    expert), 123–124
pantyhose, 129
PAR (problem, action, result)
    technique, 38
pausing, 19, 42, 117, 141
paying attention, 20–21, 42
Payscale.com (website), 74
people skills, 58
perfume, 128
permission to follow up, 96
personal branding brief, 14–15,
    44–45, 46
personal mission statement,
    answering questions about,
    57–58
personal question, being
    asked a, 88
phone follow-up, 99–101
phone screening
    automated, 25, 29–31
    live, 25, 26–29
planning, researching company,
    105–106
Plunkett, Jack (Plunkett Research,
    Ltd.), 109
Plunkett's Industry Almanacs, 110

poise, in stress interviews, 41
portfolio scam, 21
positive, being, 18
posture, 118, 120, 141
practicing for interviews
    body language, 117–120
    calming your nerves, 113–116
    discussion tips, 121
    interview traps, 121–122
    out loud, 115
    using a video recorder,
        116–117, 140
Pratfall icon, 3
pregnancy, being asked about, 88
preparing for an interview
    automated online screening, 31
    dressing the part, 123–133
    live phone screening, 26–27
    practicing body language, 117–120
    practicing discussion, 121–122
    practicing staying calm, 113–116
    practicing with a video recorder,
        116–117
    research, 103–111
    video interview, 139–140
presentation skills, answering
    questions about, 60
products or services, researching
    company, 106
provocative clothing, 129
Public Register Online (directory
    of annual reports), 108

• *Q* •

qualifications. *See also* experience
    answering questions about, 66
    in parting sales pitch, 94–95
    verifying, and targeting your
        answers to, 13–14
questions
    open and closed, 39
    screening interview, 24, 28, 30

questions, asking of interviewers.
  See also interview questions
  clarification, 47, 145
  drawing out a hidden objection,
    91–92, 94
  getting interviewer information, 35
  learning about the employer and
    job, 92, 146
  parting sales pitch, 94–95
  personal agenda, 89, 90, 92, 99
  selling yourself, 89, 90–91
  "Tell me what you want," 13
  when offered a job, 99

• R •

Raphael, Todd (editorial chief, ERE
    Media), 111
rapport, establishing, 15–16, 42
recruiter
  definition, 2
  sharing salary history with, 25
recruitment video, 111
religion, being asked about, 88
Remember icon, 3
reputation, researching company,
    106–107
research skills, answering questions
    about, 59–60
researching companies and
    industries
  fact-finding sources, 107–110, 126
  guiding questions, 105–107
  importance of, 12, 103–104
  online searching, 104
  recruitment videos, 111
  sexual orientation policy, 79
resignation, answering questions
    about, 77–78
Resumes For Dummies, 6th Edition
    (Kennedy), 14
Riley Guide's *How to Research
    Employers* (website), 108

• S •

salary
  discussing, in an interview, 16, 28,
    70–74
  discussing, with a recruiter, 25
  indicating, in an online
    application, 32
  researching your market value,
    74–75
Salary.com (website), 74
sales statement, creating a, 14–15,
    44–45, 46
scope of a position, verifying,
    13–14
screener, 2
screening interview
  about, 12–13, 23–24
  automated via computer, 31–32
  automated via phone, 7, 29–31
  live via phone, 25, 26–29
  questions, common, 24
  questions, sticky, 30
selection interview, 13, 23. *See also*
    interview; screening interview
self respect, 144
selling yourself
  through asking questions, 89–91
  interactive selling, 94
  parting sales pitch, 94–95
  in a phone screening, 27
  thank-you letter, 29, 97
serial interview, 35
service job, body language
    for a, 120
services or products, researching
    company, 106
sexual orientation, answering
    questions about, 78–80
shaking hands
  in a live interview, 119
  virtually, 138–139, 142
shirt style, 127, 128

shoes, 124, 127, 128, 130, 132
silent treatment, 122
size and growth, researching
    company, 105
skills, answering questions about,
    58–63
skirt, 124, 129
Skype, 137
small business
    approaching a, 10
    researching a, 109–110
small talk, 42
smiling, 118–119, 142
smoking, 44
social skills, importance of, 58
society membership, being asked
    about, 88
socks, 124, 128, 130
sound bite, 138–139
*Standard & Poor's Industry
    Surveys,* 110
Stewart, Jack D. (retired
    recruiter), 125
storytelling
    in answering questions about
        skills, 58–63
    in a behavior-based interview,
        36, 38
    using, 6, 10–11, 101, 143
strength, answering questions
    about a, 50
stress interview, 40–41
stressful situation, answering
    questions about a, 54
structured interview, 39
success, answering questions
    about, 53–54
suit style, 127, 128
sunglasses, 131
supervision, questions about
    working without, 68
sweater, wearing a, 129

• T •

teamwork, answering questions
    about, 53, 62–63, 67
technical check for video
    interview, 139
technology used for interviews, 7
telephone follow-up, 99–101
telephone screening
    automated, 25, 29–31
    live, 25, 26–29
tell-me-about-yourself question
    accomplishments, 49
    career objectives, 49–50
    guidelines for answering, 48
    "Is there anything else I should
        know?", 54
    in a phone screening, 28
    sales statement for answering,
        14–15
    strengths and weaknesses,
        51–53
    stressful situations, 54
    teamwork, 53
    views on success and
        failure, 53
    "Why should I hire you?", 54
tell-me-what-you-want
    question, 13
testing
    integrity, 30
    pre-employment, 19
thanks, saying, 29, 35, 96
theft of intellectual property,
    21–22
theme in personal anecdotes,
    finding a, 37–38
third-party recruiter, 2
tie style, 128, 130
time management, answering
    questions about, 61
Tip icon, 4
tiredness, 120

tone, striking the right, 27
training, answering questions about, 65–66
trapdoors, interview, 121–122
Turner, Joe (career coach), 16, 143
tutorials and guides for company research, 108

• *U* •

unemployment, answering questions about, 82–83
unexpected event, answering questions about an, 61
union membership, being asked about, 88
unsureness, 120

• *V* •

verbal skill, answering questions about, 60–61
video interview
about, 7, 135
preparing for, 139–140
successful execution, 138–139, 140–142
technology used, 136–138
video recorder, practicing with, 116–117
video resume, 142
virtual handshake, 138–139, 142
vision, personal, interview questions about, 57–58
voice, warming up
voicemail, 99–100

• *W* •

waiting for the interview, 18
watches, 131

weakness, answering questions about a, 51–53
websites
Ask Andy About Clothes, 132
company, researching on, 108, 126
Fashion.About.com, 132
Hoover's, Inc., 109–110
Indeed.com, 74
Jobstar Central, 108
LinkedIn, 109, 110
MensFashion.About.com, 132
Payscale.com, 74
Riley Guide's *How to Research Employers,* 108
Salary.com, 74
Yahoo! Finance, 108
why-did-you-apply-to-this-company question, 57
why-should-I-hire-you question, 55, 63
worker's compensation, being asked about, 88
writing skills, answering questions about, 60–61

• *Y* •

Yahoo! Finance (website), 108

• *Z* •

ZoomInfo (people search engine), 110